ASTROLOGY & FORTUNE-TELLING

ASTROLOGY
&
FORTUNE-
TELLING

DAVID V BARRETT

ACROPOLIS BOOKS

Dedicated to all those who are asking questions

© Bookmart Limited 1994

This edition first published by
Acropolis Books
Desford Road, Enderby,
Leicestershire LE9 5AD
United Kingdom

Designed, edited and produced by
Anness Publishing Limited
Boundary Row Studios
1 Boundary Row
London SE1 8HP

This edition exclusively
distributed in Canada by
Book Express, an imprint of
Raincoast Books Distribution Limited
112 East 3rd Avenue, Vancouver
British Columbia, V5T 1C8
To place orders call toll free: 1-800-663-5714

Distributed in Australia by Treasure Press

Typeset by MC Typeset Limited
Printed and bound in Singapore

ISBN 1 873762 55 0

Editorial Director: Joanna Lorenz
Project Editor: Penelope Cream
Art Director: Peter Bridgewater
Designer: Simon Balley

Contents

Astrology: Orbits of Divination

*E*verybody knows their star sign – whether or not they believe in astrology, or, indeed know anything about it at all: and nobody, however cynical, can resist turning to the 'stars' page in the newspapers or magazines to see what it says about them. It is one of the commonest collective themes in life, and a day seldom passes without astrology, the zodiac, or the stars catching the attention – either as a design motif, in advertising, on TV, or in conversation. Why would there be all this interest if there were nothing in it? Yet can we really take it seriously?

The reason that astrology permeates our lives is that it is an ancient divination system that has been with us for centuries – so much so that it has become part of our cultural furniture. The future is in the stars, and there is an enormous and proven significance in astrology and the zodiac, but these ancient truths have been buried in the devalued system popularized today.

Right: *The personifications of Mars, Mercury and Venus, and the lunar and solar symbols, from a plate in the seventeenth-century alchemical work,* Philosophia Reformata.

Introduction

Below: *An ancient map of the heavenly spheres: the figure in the centre is macrocosmic man, and the presiding woman is Astronomia. The plate is from the Shotus edition of* Margarita Philosophia.

Can the stars really foretell the future? Millions turn to their star-sign horoscope in magazines and newspapers to see what is predicted for them: this is great fun yet in reality these horoscopes are too vague and generalized to provide real guidance. Remember that you share your sign with roughly one twelfth of the population, so it is difficult to see how these nuggets of racy advice and comment can be accurate for everybody.

But there does seem to be a real truth in astrology: something that goes much deeper than a simple star sign and its generalized attributes. As in all matters of the mind, the unconscious, and hidden knowledge, the system applied will offer guidance in relation to effort invested in it. The practical guidance in this section is designed for those who wish to delve deeper than their daily newspaper predictions, to discover the secrets of their destiny by working on their own personal horoscope.

Astrology has a long and at times

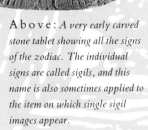

Above: *A very early carved stone tablet showing all the signs of the zodiac. The individual signs are called sigils, and this name is also sometimes applied to the item on which single sigil images appear.*

Below: *Much of the earliest recorded scholarship was inspired by the search for astrological and esoteric wisdom.*

Right: *A seventeenth-century engraving showing an early astrologer/astronomer at work with his telescope. At the beginning, astrology and astronomy were essentially one and the same thing, and even the most scientific of the observers believed that the heavens were populated by all manner of gods, beasts, and monsters.*

Above: *One of the most compelling elements of astrology – both for believers and cynics – is the incredibly rich vein of its symbolism and the beauty of its iconography. From the earliest woodcuts onwards, astrology, the zodiac and the personifications of the zodiacal signs have inspired some of the greatest artists who ever lived.*

distinguished history which – as with both dream analysis and Tarot cards, for example – is inextricably interwoven with the many religious, mythological and magical beliefs held through the ages.

The stars have always been a source of wonder to man: those familiar pinprick lights in the sky which fall so readily into familiar patterns. There is a reliable constancy about them as well, so that they have been used for navigation from earliest times.

The more man looked at the stars, the more he saw in them. And if someone is looking for signs and portents, where better to look for them? The awe and excitement that an eclipse brings even today, when we know exactly how it is caused, must have been much more powerful thousands of years ago.

The Babylonians and the Chinese especially studied the heavens, as far back as two or even three thousand years before Christ. The origins of our present astrology can be traced back to the Babylonians, although it is uncertain exactly when the division of the sky into the signs of the zodiac occurred. At one time, it is thought, there were only ten signs; at another, perhaps eighteen. At that time astrology, however it was then worked, was concerned not with the fate of individuals, but rather with the fate of the nation, or the king, which came to the same thing.

There is evidence of astrology in Egypt from the sixth century BC, and from there it was picked up by the Greeks, who did the most to codify it in a form which would be recognizable to us today.

The Greek philosophers were in advance of their time in many respects. In around 550 BC Pythagorus claimed the Earth was a sphere rather than a disc, as was then believed; and in the third century BC Aristarchus worked out that it circled the Sun, not the other way around.

However, the Greeks were not right about everything; Pythagorus (who related almost everything to music) believed the planets were attached to concentric spheres or wheels that revolved around the Earth, humming as they went. We still speak of the "music of the spheres" today, and scientists now measure the different electromagnetic vibrations of the planets. It was probably Pythagorus who worked out the idea of the octave, as well as much of the geometry still taught in schools.

Everything was interrelated: music, mathematics, the gods, the planets and stars, our individual lives. When EM Forster wrote "Only connect!" in *Howards End*, he was saying nothing new. After a couple of centuries of "rationalist" science, physicists are now saying that everything has an effect on everything else; philosophers and astrologers have been saying exactly this for thousands of years.

What the Greeks had, the Romans soon acquired; some of the greatest minds of both peoples worked on the theory and practice of astrology. It was Ptolemy (second century AD) who designed the horoscope much as we have it today. His *Tetrabiblos* or *Quadripartite*, a four-volume work, became the standard astrological textbook for centuries to come. Ptolemy was one of the first to have the troublesome thought that it would make far more sense to draw a horoscope for the moment of conception rather than birth, with the attendant problem that people very rarely know when they were conceived. Serious astrologers still find this problematic, but there is little that can be done about it.

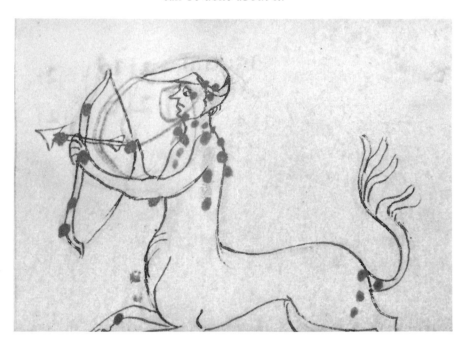

A b o v e : *A fifteenth-century constellation image of Sagittarius from a manuscript in the Bodleian Library. It shows how creative the early astrologers were in shaping such detailed figures out of a very few observable stars.*

The idea of "mundane houses" was also Ptolemy's; his "equal house" system of dividing up the horoscope is by far the simplest and most logical way of doing it; 30 degrees per sign, and no complex calculations. Over the centuries many other, more complicated ways have been developed, each claiming to be the most accurate.

The medieval Arabs were responsible for a large number of developments. One of these was Jabir ibn Hayyan, a Sufi mystic who died around AD 815, known in the West as Geber. The complexity of his many writings on magic, alchemy,

astrology and medicine has almost certainly given us the words "jabber" and "gibberish".

Part of the reason for the complexity of astrology is that the deeper we reach into any metaphysical subject, the less useful everyday language becomes; everything is symbolic of something else, and everything that can conceivably be linked together is so, with ever more abstruse connections.

The other reason, of course, is secrecy. Occult comes from a root meaning "to hide"; esoteric from a root meaning "within" (i.e. excluding outsiders); while hermetic, although coming from the cult of Hermes Trismegistus, the imaginary and mysterious god-figure associated with alchemy, has now taken on the meaning of "airtight", as in an hermetic seal.

The secrecy was for two reasons. Firstly, Christian authorities have nearly always been inimical towards anything smacking of magic. Many leading thinkers through the ages have been killed by the Church on charges of heresy; Giordano Bruno was burnt to death in 1610; even Queen Elizabeth I's astrologer John Dee came under suspicion of heresy and witchcraft. Hierarchical religions have always been hostile to and distrusted anyone who thinks independently, whether mystics with what appeared to be a direct link to God, or "magicians" who tap powers not under the control of the Church. Evangelical Christians today still view anything remotely "occult" with horror, but you can now openly buy books on Christian astrology.

The second reason for secrecy was simply human nature. If someone has worked long and hard to find out certain rare truths, these are not going to be passed around on a plate; everyone likes the feeling of knowing they know something no one else knows.

Arabic thinkers, particularly the Spanish Moors, added much to the philosophy of astrology and alchemy. One of the greatest of them, the eleventh century Ibn Ezra, came up with another way of calculating the twelve houses, modified and introduced to the West as the Regiomontanus method (the name taken by the fifteenth century German mathematician Johann Müller).

The twelfth and thirteenth centuries were, compared with both earlier and later eras in Western Europe, times of learning and the love of

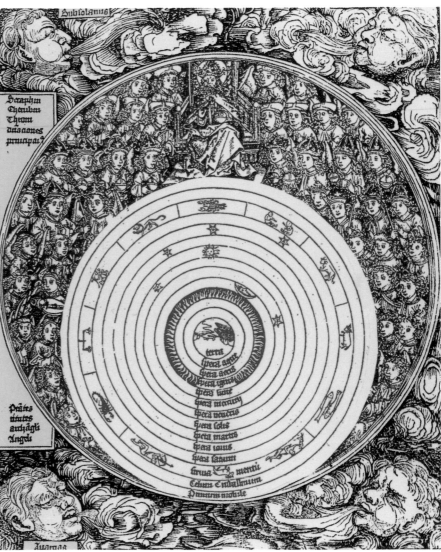

learning. Oxford University was founded in 1167, about ten years after the university at Paris. Astrology was taught as part of astronomy, and was held in high esteem by the friar-philosopher-scientist Roger Bacon, who studied in both cities. Bacon, incidentally, was a great proponent of "the scientific method" of repeatable experiments; he carried out a lot of work on optics (he invented the magnifying glass, and may have invented the telescope); he also worked out the complex system (still used today) for determining when Easter falls each year.

Bacon distinguished carefully between "natural magic" (including astrology, alchemy and medicine), which did not conflict with Christian belief, and demonic magic. Sadly, he too ended up imprisoned for heresy for fifteen years near the end of his life; he died in 1294, aged 80.

The hermetic philosophers of the seventeenth century took their name from Hermes (the Greek messenger god) Trismegistus ("the thrice-greatest"). Although an imaginary figure, he was held to be the author of more than 20,000 books. It is now thought that the books came from the hands of several writers, over several centuries, and, more than likely, several countries; but their authorship is unimportant compared to their content. It was the figure of Hermes Trismegistus who (amongst many other teachings and a variety of beliefs) codified the idea that each of the twelve zodiacal signs rules a different part of the human body.

These writings had only just surfaced in the Western world, and became source material for the alchemist-philosophers of the seventeenth century. As well as Dee and Bruno, Robert Fludd, William Lilly and the earlier Cornelius Agrippa were amongst the significant names of the period.

The hermetic philosophers, operating for the most part in secrecy, are important not just because of their discoveries and teachings, but also because they were the last people who happily mixed science and religion. A well-educated "Renaissance man" could still know just about everything that was known; the split between the sciences and the arts, and the increasing compartmentalisation of the sciences, were about to begin.

It did not matter that the Earth had now been shown to revolve around the Sun, rather than vice

Top, left: In the early years of astrology, there was no perceived conflict between astrological study and religion, as can be seen from the zodiac in the thirteenth-century nave of San Miniato al Monte, in Florence.

Above: A beautifully detailed fifteenth-century chart of the zodiac and planetary spheres, set within a crescent of the nine angelic hierarchies.

versa; this could be accepted as a fact, as one kind of truth, while for astrological purposes the Earth was still at the centre of the universe. There was no conflict; for one thing, truth was higher than fact, and for another, it was all a matter of perception anyway. The relative relationship of the Earth and Sun remained the same. (We are still perfectly happy today to speak of the Sun rising, though we know it is the Earth's rotation which has brought the Sun into view; similarly, scientists are prepared to think of light as both a wave and a particle, in different contexts.)

Astrology, alchemy, and all the magical arts very soon fell into disrepute. The eighteenth century was the "Age of Reason"; magic was superstition, and superstition was irrational; this is a view still held by many today, despite the more liberal scientific thinking of the last few decades. Popular scientific belief is always a good half century behind the forefront of scientific thought; it comes from what we were taught in school, which depends largely on what our teachers (and textbook writers) were themselves taught as students.

In 1781 Uranus was discovered, followed by Neptune in 1846 and by Pluto in 1930. Astrologers were shattered, their enemies gleeful. The old planets had developed their "personalities" over thousands of years, but what were the personalities of the new planets? Some astrologers looked at social developments in the world from around the time of each planet's discovery. Uranus thus became responsible for revolutions (America in 1776, France in 1789) and the Industrial Revolution. Neptune was held responsible for mysticism and the occult revival of the nineteenth century; and Pluto for the underworld, death, the rise of the Nazis and the atom bomb.

The names of the new planets have obviously influenced what astrologers say about them, but it has to be pointed out that the names are quite arbitrary. Uranus was originally called Herschel, after its discoverer, William Herschel, while the story about the naming of Pluto is that its discoverer asked his young daughter what name he should give the planet, and she named it after her favourite cartoon character.

However, there are some astrologers who actually believe that the names were "imposed" by the planets themselves. In any case, the idea

A b o v e : *This diagram represents the male and female elements, set against the zodiacal band.*

B e l o w : *A representation of the sign of Cancer, from a hand-coloured print in a 1496 edition of Hyginus's* Poeticon Astronomicaon.

that the planets' personalities should be determined by social developments around the time of their discovery implies that they had no astrological effect before their discovery, which is a rather silly extension of solipsist belief (for example, if a tree falls in a forest and no one hears it, does it make a sound?).

Once they knew the orbits of the new planets other astrologers, perhaps more sensibly, tracked them back in history, taking their positions into consideration in their calculations. A new question arose: should the new planets be given signs of the zodiac to rule? The previous system had been quite neat: the Sun and Moon each had one sign, and the five planets two signs each, in a logical arrangement. What now?

Uranus, Neptune and Pluto have now been given zodiacal signs, but there is still some dis-agreement about which ones they should have, and it is noticeable that they accompany, rather than supplant, the old planets in those signs.

Some astrologers, not wanting to be caught out if yet more planets are discovered (which is quite likely), have already given names – and orbits – to them. One of these, Chiron, does exist, but is actually a comet, not a planet at all. Another, Vulcan, supposedly nearer to the Sun than Mercury, has been comprehensively dis-proved. Despite this, it is possible to buy ephemerides for them.

Does astrology work? And if so, how?
....

Does astrology have any validity? Certainly some of the greatest minds in history have used it and believed in it, but the modern rationalist wants more than that.

The main difficulty with testing the claims of astrology scientifically is that there is far more to it

Left: *A delightful view of the heavens from seventeenth-century France. This chart of the constellations of the northern hemisphere was engraved for Augustine Royer.*

than simply calling someone Leo because they were born in late July or early August. An hour's difference – or much less – in birth can make a tremendous difference to a horoscope; so can a few miles' difference in birthplace.

Statistical studies have been made to both prove and disprove astrology, and the results have been ambiguous. It is always possible for critics to cast doubt on the methodology of a study, then to come up with a study of their own "proving" the opposite, which in turn is discredited.

Probably the best-known studies were carried out in the 1950s by the Frenchman Michel Gauquelin who, with very large samples, found no correlation between horoscope readings and personality, but did find significant correlations between certain factors (mainly the Moon, Mars, Jupiter or Saturn in the ascendant or descendant) and people's career choices. Many athletes and soldiers have a dominant Mars, scientists a dominant Saturn, and clergymen, actors, politicians and journalists a dominant Jupiter; the Moon appears to be responsible for writers. But the sign of the zodiac, the aspects of the planets, and the houses they lie in all appeared to be irrelevant.

Other studies, including one involving the psychologist Hans Eysenck, do appear to show correspondences, at least between the elemental

Left: *A coloured engraving showing Tycho Brahe, the Danish astrologer and so-called occultist, at work in his observatory at Uraniborg, on the island of Hveen. Brahe (1546–1601) worked at the cusp of the schism between astronomy and astrology. He is known to have cast many horoscopes and to have made predictions, while at the same time being extremely cynical about the work of other astrologers, whom he described as charlatans.*

Below: *A personal horoscope of Tycho Brahe which was cast for 13 December 1546.*

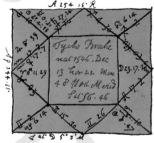

groups of signs and personality traits. Apparently neither Gauquelin nor Eysenck expected to find any "proof" that astrology works.

For those who believe in astrology, how does it work? Is it possible that the planets and stars do actually influence us at the moment of our births? It is certainly well proven that the Moon affects far more than the tides; molluscs open and shut their shells, rats become more or less active, and the behaviour of mentally disturbed people fluctuates along with the movements and phases of the Moon. Sunspot cycles have also been shown to be linked to all sorts of things on the Earth, from stock market prices to the incidence of particular diseases to, it is said, the rise and fall of hemlines.

A recent book by astronomer (not astrologer) Dr Percy Seymour, *Astrology: The Evidence of Science* (1988), argues strongly for the influence of the gravitational pull of the planets on Earth's own magnetic field, setting up resonances which affect us all our lives, but most of all in the womb.

Others prefer to accept the idea of synchronicity, a term coined by Carl Jung. Going back to the ancients, and the alchemists, "as above, so below" does not necessarily mean that "above" causes "below"; the relative positions of the planets, and the future personality of a new-born baby, may be linked because *both are aspects of the whole.*

The Signs of the Zodiac

Above: *The personification of Mercury, who rules over the symbols for Gemini and Virgo.*

Below: *This zodiacal plan of the universe shows man bound together with all the other elements of the universe – animal, vegetable, mineral, and aetherial.*

We are all familiar with our own sign, and sometimes with all twelve, but for a fuller picture it is worth examining how the signs fit together in relation to each other, before going on to examine them individually.

Twelve is a very versatile number; it can be divided by two, three, four and six, as well as, of course, by one and twelve. The numbers two and four are significant in themselves: two forms the basis of the binary system, and also makes up the fundamental elements of Eastern beliefs based on the opposites of Yin and Yang; four is the number of seasons of the year and so is associated with the natural cycle of life. Numbers underlie everything to do with astrology; numerical principles were used by the Babylonians, by Pythagorus, by the medieval Arabs and by the seventeenth century hermetic philosophers, in fact by everyone who has had anything to do with formulating astrology.

In the Western world, a complex system based

Above: *A seventeenth-century representation of the twelve sigils of the zodiacal signs, together with additional planetary sigils.*

on the number twelve was devised to account for everything we experience in life, every quality, every occurrence; it was a key to a full and deep understanding of the individual, the world, the universe; twelve is also the basis of the astrological zodiac. Some authorities have shown that even the qualities ascribed to each sign and each planet have a numerical basis, rather than simply being based on detailed observation of types of people, as

A b o v e : This stunning anatomical study by William Blake shows a mathematician from the ancient world at this work. The study of numbers, mathematical relationships and geometry lies at the heart of esoteric philosophy.

T o p , r i g h t : Mythological-style figures were very often used in early astrology to depict the personifications of the planets and other zodiacal entities.

many astrologers believe. It is thought that the idea of having twelve men in a jury was to have a fair balance of all types of man, and perhaps this may also have applied to Christ's twelve disciples.

Hemispheres

The zodiac always starts at 0 degrees, Aries. The first 180 degrees are the northern signs (remembering that north is at the bottom of the zodiac): Aries, Taurus, Gemini, Cancer, Leo and Virgo. From 180 degrees to 360 degrees are the southern signs: Libra, Scorpio, Sagittarius, Capricorn, Aquarius and Pisces.

Polarity

Half the signs are positive (sometimes known as masculine), the other half negative (or feminine), alternating from one sign to the next. The positive signs are Aries, Gemini, Leo, Libra, Sagittarius and Aquarius. The negative signs are Taurus, Cancer, Virgo, Scorpio, Capricorn and Pisces. Depending on your sign of the zodiac, the elements affecting you will, in turn, be either positive or negative.

The Elements

For thousands of years it was thought that everything was made up from four elements: earth, air, fire and water, not in a physical or chemical sense, but in the sense that the nature of everything depends on the precise mixture of elemental principles. Zodiacal signs, gods, spirits and "little people", Tarot suits, and much else are divided into these four elements. Objects, personalities, relationships and so on are made up from a balance of the four elements. (Sometimes in esoteric circles a fifth element, spirit, is mentioned, but it does not form part of the four elements of matter.)

Each element has its own attributes:

Earth: earthy, practical, solid, materialistic, constant, dependable, diplomatic, cautious, sometimes dull or suspicious.

Air: mental, intellectual, reasoning, analytic,

Right: The twelve houses, with zodiacal signs and planets, as depicted in Leonard Reymann's Nativitat Kalendar *of 1515.*

Below: In many mythologies, man and animals are merged to form fabulous new creatures.

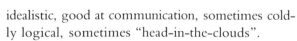

idealistic, good at communication, sometimes coldly logical, sometimes "head-in-the-clouds".

Fire: fiery, warm, sunny, idealistic, artistic, creative, energetic, excitable, passionate, headstrong, hot-headed, hot-tempered.

Water: emotional, sympathetic, deep-feeling, romantic, artistic, spiritual, receptive, sometimes hypersensitive.

Many people are clearly more one type than another, but most people are a mixture of all four; anybody who is *only* one elemental type is seriously unbalanced, while someone who is completely missing one type is lacking in one personality area. (Compare the Yin and Yang of the Chinese Tao; it is the balance which is important.)

The twelve zodiacal signs are divided between the elements:

Earth: Capricorn, Taurus, Virgo
Air: Aquarius, Gemini, Libra
Fire: Aries, Leo, Sagittarius
Water: Pisces, Cancer, Scorpio

Quadruplicities

As well as four sets of three, the signs are also divided into three sets of four, known as the quadruplicities, or qualities. The cardinal signs mark the beginning of each season, and have the idea of a new start, leadership, activity, restlessness. The fixed signs are in the middle of each season, and denote stability but inflexibility, dependability but dullness. The mutable (or common) signs mark the change from one season to the next, from the old to the new, and show flexibility and adaptability, but instability; they also show selflessness and service.

The twelve signs are divided as follows:
Cardinal: Aries, Cancer, Libra, Capricorn
Fixed: Taurus, Leo, Scorpio, Aquarius
Mutable: Gemini, Virgo, Sagittarius, Pisces

Rulers

Each sign is ruled by one of the planets, which also has its part in defining the character of the sign (see the section on Planets).

The Sun rules in Leo by day, and the Moon by night next door in Cancer. Each of the other "old" planets rules two signs, one by day, one by night, determined by how far away from the Sun the planet is. Thus Mercury's two signs are the next on either side, Virgo and Gemini; Venus rules the next two, Libra and Taurus; then Mars rules Scorpio and Aries; Jupiter rules Sagittarius and Pisces; and finally Saturn, the coldest planet, furthest away from the Sun, rules the two signs opposite to those of the Sun and Moon, Capricorn and Aquarius.

The "new" planets of Uranus, Neptune and Pluto have, according to some astrologers, become "junior partners" or co-rulers on some signs, though there is some disagreement, especially over Pluto. Other astrologers seem to have made the new planets sole rulers of the signs given to them. The signs and their planetary rulers can be listed as follows:

Aries	Mars (night) (and/or Pluto, say some authorities)
Taurus	Venus (night)
Gemini	Mercury (night)
Cancer	Moon (night)
Leo	Sun (day)
Virgo	Mercury (day)
Libra	Venus (day)
Scorpio	Mars (day) (and/or Pluto, say more reliable authorities)
Sagittarius	Jupiter (day)
Capricorn	Saturn (day)
Aquarius	Saturn (night) (and/or Uranus)
Pisces	Jupiter (night) (and/or Neptune)

All of these factors work together to determine the character of each star sign. More importantly, the combinations made by the planets lying within different signs in a horoscope, and the relationships between them all, are what determine the detailed individual interpretation of each person's birth chart.

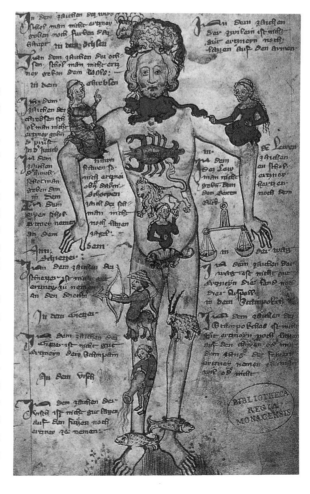

Left: *An early anatomical plan of the body, showing the areas thought to be governed by the different signs of the zodiac.*

The Signs and what they Signify

Everyone is aware of which sign of the zodiac they are born under, and which qualities it represents. There are often subtle differences in the attributed qualities, according to each astrologer's own interpretation of the other elements affecting the signs. The characteristics given here are of classic examples of each star sign. They are archetypes; very few people of any sign are exactly like these descriptions, although some may prove surprisingly accurate and relevant. Scientific and mathematical calculations are used in combination with a keen, observant eye and a strong intuitive sense to draw up a horoscope. There are certain pieces of information you need to bear in mind: as well as the Sun sign, determined by your date of birth, you should also take note of which sign is in the ascendant, which signs all the planets lie in, and how the planets relate to each other in position: in conjunction, opposition, trine and square.

Above: An engraving of the Egyptian zodiac, formerly from the Temple of Osiris.

Below: Henry Cornelius Agrippa (1486–1534) wrote some of the seminal works on occult philosophy and greatly influenced the hermetic thinkers of the sixteenth century.

Below: Seventeenth-century planetary sigils from an alchemical diagram published in 1677.

ARIES *(the Ram)*

21 March – 19 April

Northern, Positive, Cardinal, Fire, Mars (night)

The Aries person is strong, determined, forceful, a born leader. Aries people may be aggressive, domineering and irritable, perhaps even violent and destructive. They are energetic, ambitious, full of energy, full of new ideas and the drive to go out and put them into action. This drive is powered more by initial impetus than by a steady, continuing perseverance, so Aries people can be unreliable.

TAURUS *(the Bull)*

20 April – 20 May

Northern, Negative, Fixed, Earth, Venus (night)

Taurans are strong too, but in a different way. While the Ram is aggressive, the Bull has the advantage of sheer weight and solidity. They are slow, patient, and careful, but they are tenacious, and will get there in the end. They are reliable and dependable, and good family providers. They are slow to anger, but if they are provoked, stand well clear; they can have a vile and violent temper. They are extremely possessive, both in love and in their creature comforts; taken to extremes they can be gluttons and drunkards, but they can be excellent cooks.

GEMINI *(the Twins)*

21 May – 21 June

Northern, Positive, Mutable, Air, Mercury (night)

Gemini people are usually argumentative and often self-contradictory. Being both intellectual and emotional, they are likely to hold at least two different viewpoints on everything, and, being

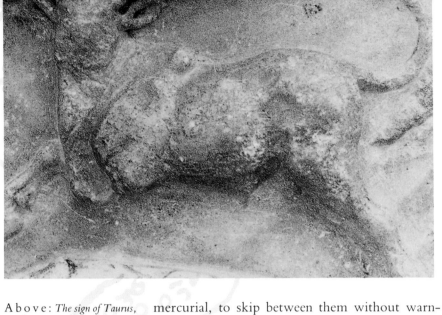

A b o v e : *The sign of Taurus, from a second-century Roman carving.*

mercurial, to skip between them without warning. They can also be very changeable in mood, going from being happy, light and carefree, to sullen and moody in a split second. They are intelligent, adaptable, inventive and versatile, and if you can take the pace, they are great fun to be with. They are charming and ingenious, and they know it; but they can turn these virtues into vices.

CANCER *(the Crab)*

22 June – 22 July

Northern, Negative, Cardinal, Water, Moon

Cancer people are sensitive (often over-sensitive), romantic, warm, gentle, considerate, protective (often over-protective) and home-loving. They are good at listening to other people's problems, but have a tendency to become over-involved; if they do not maintain a certain distance they can become "swamped" by others' emotions and problems. They also tend to hug their own problems to themselves, which can make them introspective. They often brood over their mistakes for far too long. Cancer men may have strong shoulders, but they are very sensitive, and are easily hurt by a harsh word. They may have an exaggerated sense of fair play, and can over-react if they feel they are unjustly criticized. On the other hand, they are tenacious (sometimes stubborn) and very protective, especially of those dependent on them. They possess both the good and the bad aspects of a "maternal" nature.

B e l o w : *A fifteenth-century manuscript depicting a stylized constellation image of Leo.*

LEO *(the Lion)*

23 July – 22 August

Northern, Positive, Fixed, Fire, Sun

Leos are strong, independent and masterful; they know they are natural leaders, which can make them seem proud, haughty and patronizing. They are courageous, honest and loyal, but they expect the same in return. They are also perfectionists; they set high standards and live up to them, but they expect others to do the same. They are methodical, clear-thinking and tidy-minded; they do not suffer fools. They are warm and friendly, generous and sincere, and enjoy a good social life, but they expect to be the leaders of the pack.

VIRGO *(the Virgin)*

23 August – 22 September

Northern, Negative, Mutable, Earth, Mercury (day)

Below: Scorpio, seen here in a painting on the wall of the Capitol building in Washington DC. The design was originally made by Constantino Brumidi in the nineteenth century, but it has been much restored since.

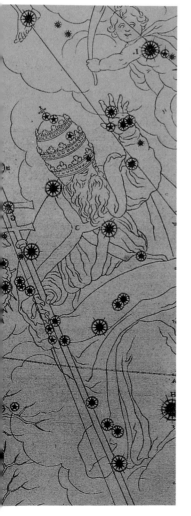

Virgo people have common sense and intelligence. At their best they can have a practical innocence; at their worst, they can be like a fussy old maid. They are quiet and dependable, not terribly creative and not great leaders. They are conscientious, neat, exact, and careful about detail: good people to whom to delegate the practicalities of organization. They tend to know themselves well, and are even more critical of themselves than they are of others. They are not great romantics, but their devotion (in love or caring) is unselfishly given. Their apparent coolness sometimes covers nervousness and tension. Their sharp intelligence often makes them quick-witted, shrewd and perceptive.

LIBRA *(the Scales)*

23 September – 23 October

Southern, Positive, Cardinal, Air, Venus (day)

Librans, like their symbol, are well-balanced people who weigh things up carefully instead of jumping to impetuous conclusions. In extreme cases they continually make comparisons, which can be undesirable. Normally, however, they are good peacemakers because they will look at all sides of a dispute, although this does sometimes mean that they are incapable of coming to a decision. They are generally diplomatic and tolerant, but can be very easily influenced by others. Their desire for peace and harmony around them also leads to a liking of beauty.

SCORPIO *(the Scorpion)*

24 October – 21 November

Southern, Negative, Fixed, Water, Mars (day) (and/or Pluto)

Scorpios are unusual and complex characters, and can be extremely powerful people. Perhaps more than those born under any other sign, they are egocentric in that they see the world through their own eyes and do not easily accept other people's points of view; they certainly will not take advice from anyone. They see everything as very clear-cut, and will come down firmly on one side or the other, with no hint of conciliation or compromise. They rarely open up their inner selves to others, and they tend to be secretive. Yet because they throw themselves into life with passion they can

Above: *Virgo as a young woman surrounded by flowers, seen in a carving on the Notre Dame Cathedral in Paris which dates from the thirteenth century.*

Top: *A copy, probably dating to the tenth century, of a zodiac from classical antiquity,*

Above: *Capricorn, as seen on the Fitzjames Arch in Merton College, Oxford.*

be compelling, almost hypnotically fascinating, to other people, and can inspire fiercely loyal friendships. There is a dark side to them: they can use their undoubted charm to their own ends. Their uncompromising attitude can be aggressive; they can be dangerous enemies to have (and they do make enemies easily), and their love life can be passionate and stormy.

SAGITTARIUS *(the Archer)*

22 November – 21 December

Southern, Positive, Mutable, Fire, Jupiter (day)

After the dark power of Scorpio, it is a relief to turn to the integrity, openness, maturity and success of the centaur-archer. Sagittarians can be just as outspoken as Scorpios, but their bluntness is without malice and rarely causes the same offence. They are full of cheerfulness, life, energy and enthusiasm, but they can show inconsistency, and impulsive anger; they often act before they think. They tend to be restless people, bounding about from one place to another (they love travel) or from one job to another. But they are honest and trustworthy, and are good teachers, if sometimes too opinionated.

CAPRICORN *(the Goat)*

22 December – 19 January

Southern, Negative, Cardinal, Earth, Saturn (day)

Capricorns make natural leaders, whether managers or politicians. They are confident, ambitious, hardworking, strong-willed and generally successful. Like the goat of their sign they will leap over obstacles or butt them out of the way, but they can also sometimes act on a capricious whim, and carelessly risk throwing everything away. However, they also remain calm and collected in difficult situations. They tend to like tradition and order, and have a "correct" way of doing things; they are deliberate, determined and practical; given these qualities, Capricorns often excel at mathematical or scientific professions. They are sometimes considered to be cold and distant because they are good at controlling their surface emotions; this can make it difficult to become close to them, but they are loyal and loving to those who are. They are also very good

Right: *A magnificent depiction of Sagittarius from a Latin manuscript in the French National Library in Paris.*

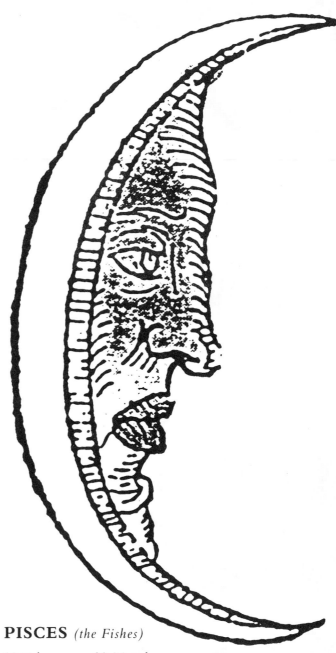

Right: *Conrad Lycosthene's extraordinary sixteenth-century vision of the Moon. Lycosthene developed the theory that there were, in fact, three Moons circulating the Earth.*

at understanding others' needs. At emotional extremes they can be overly serious, melancholic and depressive.

AQUARIUS *(the Water-Carrier)*

20 January – 18 February

Southern, Positive, Fixed, Air, Saturn (night) (and/or Uranus)

In some ways Aquarians are like a light, airy version of Scorpios, definitely without the dark side found in Scorpios, but sharing their complexity and contradictions. They attract followers because they are strong, forceful and charming, but they are quiet and well mannered. They are independent and freedom-loving, but if they sometimes shock others it is out of a sense of fun and nonconformity, or occasionally fanaticism. They are quick and bright, creative, original and artistic, sometimes wilful, sometimes conceited, arrogant and dogmatic, but also thoughtful and understanding. They enjoy company, but love their own above all. In many ways they have the archetypal virtues and flaws of the artistic genius, whether a writer, composer or painter; they also make good inventors.

PISCES *(the Fishes)*

19 February – 20 March

Southern, Negative, Mutable, Water, Jupiter (night) (and/or Neptune)

At their worst Pisces people will be aimless drifters, tossed about by the current: confused, muddled, malleable and lacking in stability. However, Pisceans are generally friendly and sympathetic. They can be keenly aware of others' emotions and feelings; if they become too receptive to these, they can be easily swayed or swamped by them. They are usually gentle, shy and retiring, but have a deep urge to help others less fortunate than themselves. They often have a strong imagination; like Aquarians they can be artistic, but they are too easily distracted.

The Planets

The patterns of the stars remain the same, but the planets wander across them; the word "planet" originally meant "wanderer". This is why, although the Sun is very clearly not a planet it can be treated as one in astrology, because it too wanders across the sky. (The Moon, although a satellite of Earth, can quite legitimately be thought of as a planet; because of the Moon's size some astronomers refer to the Earth-Moon double-planet.)

Below: Man has been fascinated by the firmament since primitive times. Every culture has developed myths and explanations which attempt to explain the movements of the heavenly bodies.

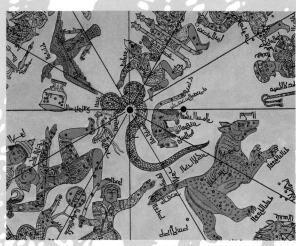

Above: Many of the greatest of the early astrologers were from Egypt and the Middle East. This detail from an Arabian map shows the constellations according to the theories of Mulhammad ben Hilal, c 1275.

It was natural that, as man created gods, he should link them with the planets, those lights that strode across the heavens. The Sun and Moon have always been objects of worship – or, to be accurate, symbols of sets of ideals which made up the character of different gods and goddesses.

The Sun gives heat and light and life; it is obviously very powerful. The Moon is cool, mysterious, changeable, the mirror of the Sun's power at night. Mercury flits around the sky as if on urgent errands: the messenger. Venus, the morning and

Right: *Sol – the Sun – personified here in the form of a god, ruling over the symbol of Leo. Sol is traditionally the bringer of life, fertility, and prosperity.*

Below: *Detail from a representation of the zodiacal sigils carved on to the Salt Tower at the Tower of London. The carving is dated 30 May 1561, and signed Hugh Draper.*

evening star, became linked with love. Mars, fiery red and aggressive in its movements around the sky, was warlike. Jupiter was stately, strong, constant: authority, but big-hearted. Saturn was much paler, slower: dying and death.

Gustav Holst's suite *The Planets* is a marvellous evocation of the characters of the planets and, like the planets themselves, it is both inspiring and awe-inspiring.

The Sun

The Sun is the largest, brightest, and most powerful object in the heavens. The Aztecs and Incas of Central America built vast cities, containing temples and observatories from which to worship and observe the Sun, which they considered most holy. Solar deities have usually (though not quite

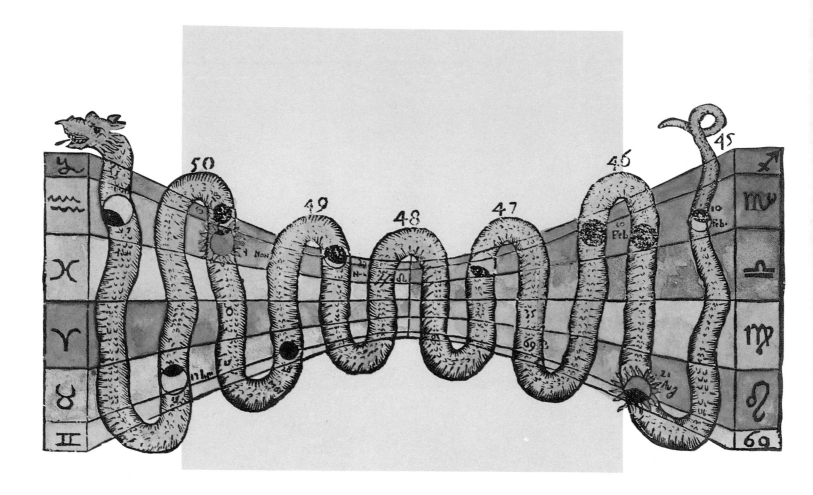

always) been male, and obviously connected with the seasons of the year. It is the Sun's position in the zodiac at our birth which gives us our "star sign" of Gemini, Cancer, Libra, Aries and so on. Solar eclipses, when the Sun is blotted out for a while, have always been portents of great disaster.

Astrologically there has been disagreement amongst the authorities whether the Sun rules the outside of a person and the Moon the inside, or the other way around. Generally, though, the Sun stands for the conscious mind, the real essence of the ego. We speak of people having a sunny disposition; generosity and faithfulness are Sun attributes, but the Sun also implies strength, power and dignity.

The Sun gave his name to Sunday, the first day of the week and the Christian holy day.

The Sun rules Leo.

The Moon

The Moon takes around twenty-eight days to orbit the Earth.

The Moon runs close to the Sun in importance. She lights up the night; she rules the tides, and all things watery; she changes through the month, giving her an obvious link, through menstruation, to the eternal female. Moon deities are almost invariably female. She has long been associated with all things mysterious, and with the subconscious mind. She also has an effect on madness (hence the words "lunatic" and "lunacy"), as pointed out by Paracelsus in the sixteenth century (though believed long before this), and confirmed by psychiatrists today.

The Moon gave her name to Monday.

The Moon rules Cancer.

Above: *This image shows the lunar dragon (combining the Caput and the Cauda associations) set against the twelve divisions of the constellational zodiac.*

Opposite: *Luna – the Moon – represents mystery and intrigue as well as intuition and sensitivity.*

Mercury

The planet Mercury takes only eighty-eight days to orbit the Sun.

Mercury, who races around the sky, is the Roman messenger of the gods, the equivalent of the Greek Hermes. He is often depicted as having wings on his feet. He is the god of childhood. Astrologically, he denotes intelligence, memory and communication, a quick-witted nature – but "mercurial", in that he will flit from whatever (or whoever) catches his attention at one moment to the next, so he is not always dependable. He is generally described as the patron of both business-men and thieves – profitable, but living on the speed of his wits.

Mercury gave his name to "mercredi" in French and "mercoledí" in Italian; "Wednesday" is named after the Norse-Germanic god Odin or Wotan, the All-Father, who is somewhat more important in the hierarchy of gods than Mercury, but shares his attributes of wisdom and energy, and, similarly, also represents thieves, as well as those involved in business and marriage deals.

Mercury rules the two signs closest to those of the Sun and Moon: these are Virgo by day, and Gemini by night.

Venus

The planet Venus takes two hundred and twenty-five days to orbit the Sun.

Venus is the Roman goddess equivalent to Aphrodite, the earlier Greek goddess of love, beauty, peace and harmony. She is the essence of the female (her symbol is the universal scientific symbol for female or feminine). She is also the goddess of youth or adolescence. Venus governs the emotions, and also æsthetics, the appreciation of beauty.

The word venereal, now usually only associated with sexual diseases, in fact means anything to do with sexual intercourse; venery is sexual indulgence. It should always be remembered that all the planets and gods, like all the zodiacal signs, contain both good and bad. Sensuality and passion are natural and healthy feelings, but because they are so powerful, they can be mis-directed. Over-indulgence in the gratification of pleasure can be associated with Venus – as can indolence.

Right : Here a rustic figure, inspired by the music and cosmic influence of the stars and zodiac symbols, is playing the bagpipes. This is a plate from a late fifteenth-century Shepherd's Calendar.

Venus gave her name to "vendredi" in French and "venerdí" in Italian; "Friday" is named after the Norse-Germanic goddess Freyja, or more likely Frigg, whose symbol, the distaff (or spinning-stick), has become the term for the female side of the family.

Venus, the next planet out from the Sun after Mercury, rules the next two signs out: Libra by day and Taurus by night.

Mars

The planet Mars takes six hundred and eighty-seven days to orbit the Sun.

Mars is the Roman god of war and battle, but not necessarily of aggression; here he differs from the nearest Greek equivalent, Ares, who was a lot more bloodthirsty, and not a popular god at all. Mars' strength, like any good soldier's, is disciplined, and he is likely to attack in order to defend, rather than for conquest. Mars has given us the word martial, meaning to do with warfare.

He is honourable, courageous, active and energetic – and is seen as the universal symbol for male or masculine. Modern astrologers often say that if Venus is love, Mars is sex, but this is far too

Imagine di Venere nata dalla spuma del mare, della bellez-
za Dea, & della libidine, madre d'Amore, simbolo della la-
sciuia, qual sù anco tenuta Dea delse nozze & del matrimo-
nio, intesa per il pianeta di Venere, detta ancor Lucifero, &
Hespero, che induce la virtù generatiua nelle cose.

magini de Tritoni & delle Nereide huomini & donne mari
ne secondo Alessandro Napolitano, Theodoro Gaza, & alr
ntichi, & moderni; con l'imagine di Galatea nereide prin-
oale, & suo carro significante la doppia virtù delle acque.

A b o v e : *Two visions of Venus, after the style of Lorenzo Pignoria Padonvo, from his book* Le Vere e Nove Imaginini de gli Dei delli Antichi, *which was produced in Padua in 1615. Venus is seen being born out of the sea spray; she is in the traditional pose on the half-shell. In astrological terms, she represents love, sensuality and desire.*

simplified. In the ages of man, Mars is the young adult.

Mars gave his name to "mardi" in French and "martedí" in Italian; "Tuesday" is named after the Norse-Germanic god Tyr, the defender-god.

Mars, the next planet out from the Sun, after Venus, rules the next two signs out: Scorpio by day and Aries by night.

Jupiter

The planet Jupiter takes nearly twelve years to orbit the Sun.

Jupiter is mature and expansive, good-hearted and merciful, majestic and magnificent. He is powerful, and he can be dangerous; his thunderbolts have been known to miss. He is the mature adult, the successful businessman; he denotes prosperity and good fortune, order and organization. He is associated with good health, and his symbol is still used to denote medicine.

The **Roman** god Jove, who is equated with the Greek god Jupiter, has given us the word jovial, meaning convivial or big-hearted.

Jupiter's Roman equivalent Jove gave his name to "jeudi" in French and "giovedí" in Italian; "Thursday" is named after the Norse-Germanic god Thor, the god of thunder.

Jupiter, the next planet out from the Sun, afte Mars rules the next two signs out: Sagittarius by day and Pisces by night.

Saturn

The planet Saturn takes twenty-nine and a half years to orbit the Sun.

Saturn, the furthest away of the "old" planets, is seen as dark, gloomy, melancholy and sluggish, the very essence of our word "saturnine". In contrast with Jupiter's expansiveness, Saturn is limiting. He will slow down enterprises, turning success into failure. He personifies old age, which includes wisdom and teaching as well as lameness and decrepitude.

The Roman god Saturn was originally the Roman god of agriculture, especially corn, so he wielded a sickle. So did the Greek god Cronos (or Kronos), but he used his to castrate his father

Uranus, and then ate his own children – not one of the most pleasant deities. The Romans then further confused Cronos with "chronos", the Greek word for time. So Saturn has become identified with the Grim Reaper, Old Father Time, scything down lives. The nearest equivalent of the original Roman god Saturn is actually the Greek goddess of vegetation (especially corn), Demeter, one of the children of Cronos.

Saturnalia was a Roman mid-winter festival when slaves were allowed to run free, and everyone indulged in drunkenness and orgies; the Lord of Misrule, a mock king, was allowed absolute licence. This chaotic but fun aspect of Saturn is

Below: *The planets personified, and set inside a zodiacal border.*

unfortunately often forgotten by astrologers.

Saturn gave his name to "Saturday".

Saturn, the next planet out from the Sun after Jupiter, rules the next two signs out: Capricorn by day and Aquarius by night.

The "new" planets

It should be remembered that these planets had no part in traditional astrology; their characteristics have only been developed over the last couple of centuries for Uranus, and the last few decades for Pluto. The choice of their names has also not had the blessing of time, although many astrologers work backwards from these names to ascribe astrological attributes to the planets.

How much weight should be put upon them is up to the individual. They are far away, and cannot be seen with the naked eye; whatever effects they have might be very weak. Also, because of the length of their orbits, there would be little appreciable difference from year to year, let alone from minute to minute.

On the other hand, if the planets in our solar system *do* have an effect on our lives, then so must these three, and the ancients simply did not know about them. But in deciding what effects they might have, we are denied the accumulated wisdom of millennia.

Uranus

The planet Uranus, discovered in 1781, takes eighty-four years to orbit the Sun – and seven years to pass through a single sign of the zodiac.

The god Uranus was the Greek sky-god castrated and deposed by his son Cronos. His other children included the Titans and the Cyclopes, so he can be seen as the father of disruption. He was the god of lightning, so astrologers have given him electricity to look after.

We have already seen that many astrologers believe that Uranus is responsible for political revolutions and industrial development – social changes rather than personal ones. Some equate revolutions with disruption, others with democracy and international collaboration. In individual terms, this could mean originality, unconventionality and invention.

Uranus has been given Saturn's night sign, Aquarius, to rule.

A b o v e : *An early map from late-Roman antiquity depicting the constellations, with personifications of the Sun and the Moon and the zodiacal asterims.*

Neptune

· ·

The planet Neptune, discovered in 1846, takes one hundred and sixty-five years to orbit the Sun; nearly fourteen years per zodiacal sign.

The god Neptune was the Roman god of the sea (equivalent to the Greek god Poseidon), so many astrologers ascribe watery characteristics (previously the province of the Moon) to the planet. Some say he represents "whatever dissolves", and so by inference anything vague and undefined, including alcohol and drugs. He is thought to signify, in his more negative state, deception and whatever may be illusory in a character or situation. He is also given the spiritual and mystical aspects of the Moon's personality.

Because of the idea of water, some astrologers give Neptune Jupiter's night sign, Pisces, to rule.

Pluto

· ·

The planet Pluto, discovered in 1930, takes two hundred and forty-eight years to orbit the Sun – over twenty years per sign of the zodiac. Although known as the furthest planet, Pluto's orbit is so eccentric that for the rest of this century it will be closer to the Sun than Neptune is.

Pluto is another name for Hades, the Greek god of the underworld. It was said to bring bad luck to use the name Hades, so the god had various pseudonyms, including Pluton, meaning "the rich" (hence the word plutocracy, rule by the wealthy). Most astrologers seem to be drawing the planet's astrological personality from the idea of the underworld: the dark side of mankind, death and transformation.

Some astrologers give Pluto Mars's day sign, Scorpio, to rule; others seem to prefer Pisces, which most assign to Neptune; one astrologer even says Aries, presumably on the grounds that it is the next one round after Neptune's Pisces, though Aries and Mars are so closely linked that most astrologers would find it unimaginable to separate them. It is not unusual for there to be varying opinions amongst astrologers and differences of viewpoint often occur.

Presumably if another two planets are discovered, they will each be given one of Venus's and Mercury's two signs.

Opposite : An allegory for the perfection of humanity, with the zodiacal signs both within and around the figure: the whole illustrates the relationship between the microcosm and the macrocosm.

A b o v e : *The seven planets shown in a schema (pattern, or plan) of roundels, from an illumination of c 1400. The original is in the British Museum. The plate is of interest, reminding us that medieval astrology comprised a complex system which functioned, of course, without the planets Neptune and Pluto. The discovery of these planets, in the nineteenth and twentieth centuries respectively, dismayed astrologers, who had to quickly revise and re-evaluate their methodology, and determine whether or not these new bodies could be legitimately incorporated into the astrological philosophy.*

The Horoscope

A horoscope is a schematic map of the heavens at a specific moment – usually, but not necessarily, the moment of someone's birth. In fact, natal astrology is a relatively late development, from around the fifth century BC.

Horoscopes can also be drawn up for countries, and even for companies; this is known as mundane astrology, and appears to predate natal astrology considerably.

Horary astrology uses the horoscope by taking an astrological snapshot of the moment the question is asked in order to give an answer to the question.

A progressed horoscope looks at an individual's future; in the most widely-known system the astrologer takes the birthchart and progresses it by a day for each year of the subject's life. To draw a horoscope for someone's fortieth birthday, he would, by this system, set it exactly forty days after the moment of birth; but this is only one of several ways of doing it, and many serious astrologers dismiss the idea altogether.

Electional astrology, on the other hand, has considerable support; it calculates planetary positions for given moments in the future, to find the most propitious time for a proposed important activity: a political conference, or the laying of a foundation stone, for example.

Astrology is still used medically (though rarely by "orthodox" Western doctors) to help indicate imbalances in the body. The fourth-fifth century BC Greek physician Hippocrates (after whom the medical Hippocratic oath is named) claimed it was essential for doctors to be able to interpret a horoscope.

Although we now know that the Earth, and all the other planets, orbit the Sun, for the purposes of astrology the Sun, the Moon and the planets are treated as if they orbit the Earth – which is, of course, what they appear to do. This does not automatically invalidate astrology: it is the relationship of the heavenly bodies that is important, rather than the physical position of a hunk of rock or ball of gas.

Looking up at the sky (from the northern hemisphere) we see the old familiar constellations: the Plough, Cassiopeia, Orion. If we know what to look for (and constellations are by no means obvious) we can pick out the twelve constellations which make up the zodiac. (The word zodiac comes from a Greek root meaning "circle of animals"; many of the zodiacal constellations are animals.) These all lie in one wide belt across the sky, in which the Sun and Moon also appear.

As the Earth pursues its orbit around the Sun these twelve constellations march along their path during the course of the year, which is why they made a useful calendar for the ancients. The circle of the sky, 360 degrees, divided by twelve, gives 30 degrees for each sign of the zodiac, and roughly one degree per day of the year. Each sign, though it spans two months, therefore lasts about 30 days.

Wandering among the constellations are the planets and the Moon. Although the brightness of the Sun blots out its backdrop of stars, the constellations are still behind it, and the Sun's path can be plotted across them as if it were a planet.

Because of the tilt of the Earth's axis (at an angle of 23 degrees, 27 minutes to its orbital plane), the noon Sun rises higher in the sky in summer than in winter; the summer solstice, around 21 June, is its highest point, where it

Once the basics of astrology are understood, it takes its place amongst the great systems of self-enlightenment and divination, such as those illustrated here – palm-reading, geomancy, and Tarot – and others like dream interpretation, I Ching and runes. Astrologers, such as the medieval scholar shown, bottom right, have been predicting future events for hundreds of years.

Knight of Cups

Right: *A beautiful constellation map illustrating the planetary movements according to the Copernican heliocentric (Sun-centred) system, c 1661.*

appears to pause before sliding back down the sky through autumn and into winter. The winter solstice, the Sun's low pausing point, is around 22 December. So, the Sun is in the sky for longer in the summer than in the winter; day is longer in summer, night is longer in winter. The spring and autumn equinoxes, around 20–21 March and 22–23 September, are the mid-points at which day and night are exactly equal. The solstices and equinoxes have, from earliest times, been major religious festivals.

The Zodiac and the Constellations

The horoscope notionally shows exactly where each planet (including the Sun and the Moon) is against the constellations behind it. This indication is notional because the position of the zodiacal constellations in the sky today is not the same as the astrological zodiacal signs. As well as being

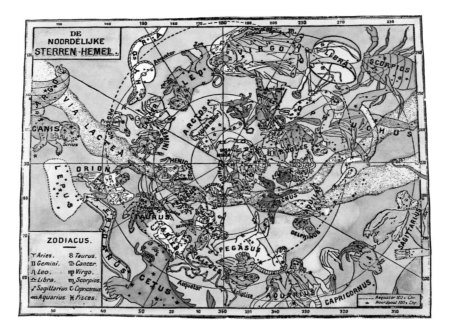

Right: *A relatively modern, c 1919, Dutch constellation chart after the edition of Libra's* Astrology – Its Techniques and Ethics. *The map places the animals of the zodiac in their places in the heavens.*

Below: *A charming eighteenth-century constellation map printed for Gerald Valk and Peter Schenk. The breadth and quality of astrological imagery, as evidenced by the planetary and constellation charts shown on these two pages, is extraordinary. These pieces are now widely and seriously collected as artefacts in their own right, and can fetch large sums at auction.*

tilted, the Earth also wobbles on its axis, like a spinning top, and over the centuries the direction in which its axis is pointing has changed.

When the zodiac was first drawn up, some four thousand years ago, the Sun was just entering the constellation of Aries at the point of the spring equinox. The circle of the zodiac therefore began at 0 degrees Aries on around 21 March, and progressed through the signs during the year until it reached 30 degrees Pisces on around 20 March.

The Greek astronomer Hipparchus was the first to point out, around 120 BC, that this was no longer the case. By then, the Sun was moving out of Aries into Pisces; by now, another two thousand years later, it has moved on again, and is passing out of Pisces into Aquarius.

The position of the twelve signs on a horoscope is thus "out" by two, compared with the actual position of the twelve zodiacal constellations in the sky.

Critics of astrology claim that this "precession of the equinoxes" completely invalidates the whole thing; someone whom we call Scorpio because of their birth date ought really to have the characteristics ascribed to Virgo, which are quite different. The planets that we carefully place in certain signs in the horoscope ought to be somewhere else entirely. Astrologers, in response, say that the principles remain the same, and that the horoscope is a *symbolic* representation; it does not claim to be a photographic map.

The precession of the equinoxes has given us the terms "the Age of Aries", "the Age of Pisces", and the now famous "Age of Aquarius" which we are about to enter (or, according to some astrologers, have already entered).

It may be entirely coincidental that Christianity, one of whose symbols is the fish, began at the start of the Age of Pisces, but astrologers and new agers in general have made a lot of this. We are moving, they say, from the age of confusion and instability to the age of freedom of thought and brightness of attitude.

Drawing up a horoscope

Anyone wishing to construct their own horoscope from scratch should buy a book dealing with this in full detail, and also a copy of *Raphael's Ephemeris* or any other ephemeris (plural,

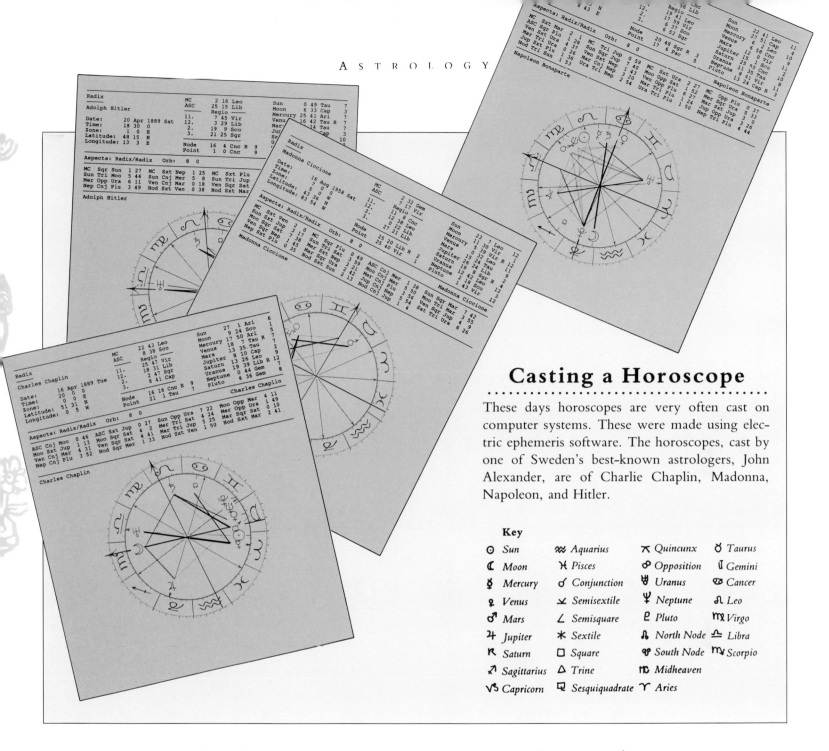

Casting a Horoscope

These days horoscopes are very often cast on computer systems. These were made using electric ephemeris software. The horoscopes, cast by one of Sweden's best-known astrologers, John Alexander, are of Charlie Chaplin, Madonna, Napoleon, and Hitler.

Key

☉ Sun	♒ Aquarius	⚻ Quincunx	♉ Taurus		
☾ Moon	♓ Pisces	☍ Opposition	♊ Gemini		
☿ Mercury	☌ Conjunction	♅ Uranus	♋ Cancer		
♀ Venus	⚺ Semisextile	♆ Neptune	♌ Leo		
♂ Mars	∠ Semisquare	♇ Pluto	♍ Virgo		
♃ Jupiter	✳ Sextile	☊ North Node	♎ Libra		
♄ Saturn	□ Square	☋ South Node	♏ Scorpio		
♐ Sagittarius	△ Trine	⚷ Midheaven			
♑ Capricorn	⚼ Sesquiquadrate	♈ Aries			

ephemerides) which gives the position of the Sun, Moon and every planet at different times on every day of the year. Whatever the times given in the tables, you can be sure that the exact time of your birth – which is what you need – will fall somewhere between them, which means you have to take the planetary positions at the nearest time, work out (for each planet) how far it will have travelled between then and your birth time, and add or subtract the degrees and minutes.

Before you can do any of this you need to know the exact longitude of your birthplace, so that you can convert the local time of your birth to Greenwich Mean Time (GMT). You also, of course, have to remember to take into account local variations such as British Summer Time or Daylight Saving Time.

All these mathematical workings-out can be very complicated, which is why many astrologers now use, and recommend, a computer program. There is absolutely no reason why not; after all, constructing a horoscope is nothing more than calculating what is where, when.

Do *not*, however, take note of any computer program which then goes on to "interpret" the horoscope for you. Interpretation is largely a matter of instinct and intuition which computers as yet do not possess. You will also need to know the ascendant and the *medium coeli*.

The ascendant is the sign which was rising on the eastern horizon at your moment of birth; this is almost as significant a factor in interpretation as your basic star sign. You not only need to know which sign it was, but how far it had "risen", so

A b o v e : *This image, after Leonard Reymann's early sixteenth-century woodcut, depicts the twelve houses of the horoscope, which appear in red.*

O p p o s i t e : *A delightfully simplistic seventeenth-century schema – almost in the style of a needlework sampler – showing the twelve houses of the zodiac and their meanings.*

the ascendant will be in the form of 8 degrees Cancer or 15 degrees Aquarius.

The *medium coeli* (MC) is the mid-heaven, the degree of the sign which was on the meridian, or due south, at that moment; again, this is in the form of 12 degrees Gemini or 23 degrees Libra. The *medium coeli* and ascendant are marked on the chart, followed by the houses.

The Houses

The astrological chart is divided into twelve sections, or houses. They represent the divisions of what is visible from Earth at any place and at any time. Also shown are the "invisible heavens", what is concealed beneath the Earth at the same time and from the same place. The houses do not have individual names but are allotted numbers. There is no one "correct" way of dividing up the horoscope into these houses. There are at least half a dozen completely different house systems in fairly wide use, all giving different results from the same data – as well as many others, less well-known. Although astrology is a complicated process and there are many variations of division and differences of opinion as to the exact positioning of houses, astrologers do agree on their meanings. Each house signifies one area of life, as follows:

1. The individual's appearance, temperament and overall potential.
2. Possessions and money.
3. Intelligence and close relationships.
4. Home, family affairs, parents.
5. Procreation, sexual relationships and pleasure, other pleasures.
6. Employees, hard work, chores.
7. Marriage, married partner, business partnerships.
8. Death, inheritance and secret wishes.
9. Expansion and exploration of the spirit and the mind; travel.
10. Career, ambition, reputation, honours.
11. Friendships, social life, associations and clubs.
12. Secrecy, the inner self, troubles, betrayals.

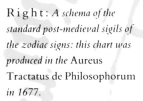

Interpretation

Whichever method is used for setting up the houses, once the framework is established all the planets (including, most importantly, the Sun and the Moon) can be put in place, with the degrees and minutes of each one. These show how the planets relate to each other.

With everything in place, the most difficult part of the whole business can begin: interpreting the horoscope. Again, there are many books which deal with this in far more detail than we can here, including long explanations of every planet in every sign, but we can outline the most significant factors to look for to obtain a meaningful reading. Different astrologers may take these in different orders, but the important thing to remember is this:

Nothing should be taken in isolation. You are looking for the overall picture. Any individual factor, however important, can be strengthened or weakened or otherwise affected by others.

1. The Sun. The sign this lies in is your "star sign"; this sign is the basic shape, the underlying foundation, of your personality. If it is in Leo, which the Sun rules, these qualities will be espe-

Left: *A highly stylized constellation map showing the places of the animals and other figures in the heavens. The artist has depicted all the constellations in a rather distorted and monstrous form. The close proximity of the astrologers to the firmament they are observing may be a metaphor for the huge influence the stars have in the life of Everyman.*

Below: *A medieval melothesic figure depicting a human form, and illustrating the qualities of the corresponding zodiacal signs. The text is Latin, and the plate almost certainly comes from a late fourteenth-century or early fifteenth-century treatise.*

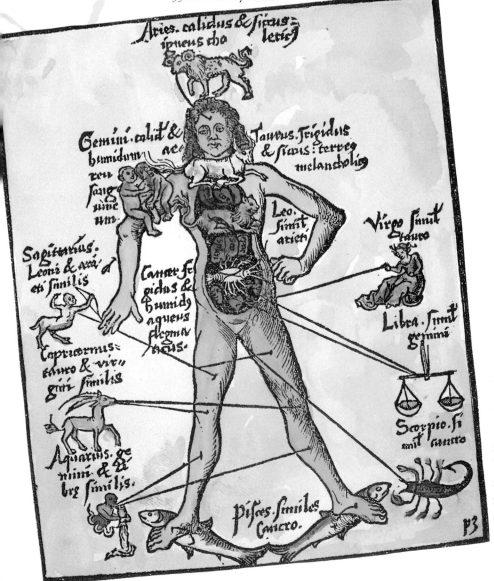

cially strong. The same applies, to a lesser extent, in the other two fire signs.

2. The Moon. This shows the characteristics of your subconscious – or, depending on terminology, your soul or spirit – the deepest, inner part of you. She governs your emotional responses, and represents all that is moving and changeable. It follows that the Moon has her strongest effect in water signs, most of all Cancer, which she rules.

3. The Ascendant. Often called the Rising Sign, the positioning of this sign indicates your temperament and instinctive attitude. Some astrologers also believe it gives an indication of your physical appearance, though quite obviously not all those with Taurus rising are short and plump with dark curly hair, and not all those with Sagittarius in the ascendant are tall and athletic-looking with a long nose!

4. The Ruling Planet. This is the ruler of the Rising Sign, the sign in which the ascendant lies. The Ruling Planet is one of the most important signifiers of character in the whole horoscope; indeed, it could be said to rule the horoscope. Where it lies – both the sign and the house – should be studied carefully, and it should be kept in mind throughout the interpretation.

A b o v e : *This wonderful image from an early German woodcut could be an allegory for the pursuit of astrology. A scholar tears his way through the walls of the firmament to discover the mechanical workings of the stellar system.*

R i g h t : *Mars, seen ruling Scorpio and Aries, and dominating a battlefield scene typical of his war-like attributes.*

5. The Elements: Fire, water, air and earth. For the rare fully-balanced person, the planets should be scattered amongst all the signs. If they are mainly in signs of just one element, then you are likely to be fiery and energetic, or earthy and practical, or quick-witted and imaginative, or emotional and intuitive. If you do not have any planets in a particular element, then you will lack those qualities.

6. The Quadruplicities. The same idea applies. If the planets are mainly in cardinal signs you are likely to be strongly self-motivated, with leadership qualities. If they are mainly in fixed signs you may be solid but stolid, dependable but obstinate. If mainly mutable, you will be very adaptable, but can be selfish. Naturally, most people are some sort of mixture, but lacking one of them altogether shows a definite weakness in that quality.

7. The Planets in the Signs. Each planet has its own personality, each sign its own character. If any planet is in the sign it rules, those qualities will be strengthened: Mars in Aries, for example. Some planets and signs get on well together; others clash, and are weakening. Some combinations are particularly worrying: slow-moving Saturn in strong-willed Scorpio denotes great seriousness and heavy responsibilities. Many astrologers put special emphasis on where Mercury lies because of its speed and agility, and what it can show about your mind and your abilities.

There are seven "old" planets (including the Sun and Moon) and twelve signs; the eighty-four individual combinations would take up a number of pages. A quick bit of mathematical calculation shows that the total number of different combinations of all the planets in all the signs comes to 12^7, or 35,831,808 different personality types – a far cry from the standard complaint of the unin-formed sceptic that according to astrology there are only twelve types of people! If you include the three "new" planets (and there are very good arguments both for and against) the total number of combinations comes to 12^{10}, or nearly sixty-two billion.

Obviously many of the combinations of planets in signs cancel each other out, and some are clearly far stronger and more significant than others. The factors already mentioned are crucial to determining the balance of the horoscope, as are two others.

8. The Aspects. The aspects are the angles between the various planets in the horoscope, and the interpretation depends a great deal on just which planets they are. Again the fundamental mathematical basis of astrology is highlighted. The main relationships are conjunction, opposition, trine, square and sextile.

Conjunction: two planets are very close – within seven degrees of each other. They combine their influences, intensifying whatever is good or bad.

Opposition: 180 degrees apart, ± 3.5 degrees. Again they combine their effects, but as they are pulling in opposite directions, this is usually bad.

Trine: 120 degrees apart, ± 3 degrees. If two planets are in trine, they reduce each other's influence in a good way, but if three are in a grand trine with each other, there is tremendous stability and balance.

Square: 90 degrees apart, ± 3 degrees. They diminish each other's effect in a bad way; if a third planet makes up a third corner of the square it is also in opposition to the first, and the overall relationship is very disruptive.

Sextile: 60 degrees apart, ± 3 degrees. This is generally favourable, in that the planets are seen to be working well with each other. It applies particularly to mental characteristics.

There are several other, less important aspects: semi-sextile (30 degrees), semi-square (45 degrees), quintile (72 degrees), sesqui-square or sesquadrate (135 degrees), bi-quintile (144 degrees) and quincunx (150 degrees). Generally, if the aspect divides the circle by 3, 5, 6 or 12, it is good; if it divides it by 2, 4 or 8 it is bad.

9. The Houses. The presence of a planet in a mundane house means that its influence will be especially felt in that area of life, either for good or for bad.

Popular astrologers often place an undue emphasis on this area of interpretation, probably because (compared with most other areas) it is relatively easy to make apparently clear (but actually vague) pronouncements: "You will be happy in love", "You will be successful in business", "Someone close to you will betray you", and so on.

Considering the disagreements amongst the experts, it is probably unwise to put too much faith in this part of the interpretation. There is a great deal of discussion about a planet being "on the cusp"; if astrologers would only agree about where the cusps (the dividing lines between the houses) actually are, this might make more sense.

10. In addition, the closeness of a planet to the ascendant or the descendant (180 degrees away),

A b o v e : *A copperplate engraved constellation chart by Andreas Cellarius, 1660. It originally appeared in Schiller's* Atlas seu Harmonia Macrocosmica *in 1660.*

gůt — mittel — böß
gůt — mittel — böß
gůt — mitttel — böß
gůtt — mittel — böß

¶Der wyder bedeütet das haubte. vnnd der
ochße den halß. als du vindeſt in der vorderen
igur gar klärlichen.

Above: *The twelve images of the zodiac signs. This hand-coloured print appeared in a German textbook on astrology c 1510.*

Right: *This is an astrological year chart, showing the various seasonal tasks that are carried out at different times and the zodiacal signs that therefore govern them. In the centre are personifications of summer and winter. This is a late fifteenth-century woodcut.*

or to the *medium coeli* at the top or the *imum coeli* at the bottom, or its presence (or more especially, the presence of several planets) in any of the quarters of the circle made by the lines drawn between these points – all these have significance.

The most important part of any interpretation, though, is the intuition of the astrologer. All the mathematical jugglings in a horoscope only point to potentialities; it is the astrologer's job to tease out the meaning.

One other vital point must be made. A horoscope does not, will not and cannot tell you what *will* happen to you in your life. It can paint a picture, of greater or lesser accuracy, of the qualities that make you the person you are; it is up to you to take those qualities, both good and bad, and make something of them.

Chinese Systems

Most Westerners think that Chinese astrology simply gives you a symbolic animal depending on which year you were born; but this is just as wrong as saying that you are a Cancer or a Leo and thinking that that is all there is to Western astrology. Chinese astrology is every bit as complicated to work out, both in the mathematical calculations and in the interpretation of the results.

Here we can unfortunately give only the basics, but even this much will show something of the richness of Chinese astrology.

It is said that one New Year the Buddha called all the animals to him, but only twelve came. To each of these in turn he gave a year to express its personality.

It is important to realize that the year has the characteristics of the symbolic animal, not just a person born in that year. Certain years are therefore more or less auspicious for beginning a new building, for example, or starting any major new

Above and left: *These three figures are from a set of Chinese domino cards. This set uses as its theme the characters from the famous Chinese tale* The Story of the River's Bank. *Just as with Tarot in the West, these Chinese pieces are games-playing devices as well as part of a divination system.*

Right: *An image of the double dragon, set between the Moon and the Sun, and standing on the Earth. There is an association between this figure and the lunar dragons of early astrology and alchemy.*

project. For individual people, the significance lies in the interplay between their own birth-year animal and that of the year in question. Some combinations are particularly fortuitous, others far less so, which is why people say they have had a good or a bad year. Your own year, every twelve years, provides excellent opportunities for your personality to flourish; the time is right for you.

Relationships obviously also depend on how the symbolic animals of each person interact with each other, and, traditionally, Chinese young men would present the details of their birth to the father of their intended young woman, who would see whether there would be a good match or not.

Chinese astrology is based on the cycles of the Moon, not those of the Sun, planets and stars. Because the lunar calendar does not fit in at all exactly with the solar calendar, the Chinese New Year is on a different date each year.

The year of each animal begins on the date in January or February shown in this chart.

Rat	24/1/36	10/2/48	28/1/60	15/2/72	2/2/84
Ox	11/2/37	29/1/49	15/2/61	3/2/73	20/2/85
Tiger	31/1/38	17/2/50	5/2/62	23/1/74	9/2/86
Cat/Rabbit	19/2/39	6/2/51	25/1/63	11/2/75	29/1/87
Dragon	8/2/40	27/1/52	13/2/64	31/1/76	17/2/88
Snake	27/1/41	14/2/53	2/2/65	18/2/77	6/2/89
Horse	15/2/42	3/2/54	21/1/66	7/2/78	27/1/90
Sheep/Goat	5/2/43	24/1/55	9/2/67	28/1/79	15/2/91
Monkey	25/1/44	12/2/56	29/1/68	16/2/80	4/2/92
Rooster	13/2/45	31/1/57	17/2/69	5/2/81	23/1/93
Dog	2/2/46	16/2/58	6/2/70	25/1/82	10/2/94
Pig	22/1/47	8/2/59	27/1/71	13/2/83	31/1/95

Over: *It is important to note that the Dragon is the only mythological animal among the twelve that make up the Chinese zodiac. Its inclusion probably dates back to its role in ancient Chinese astronomy.*

The usual criticism levelled at Chinese astrology (similar to the one levelled at Western astrology), that it says that everyone born in a particular year is of one type out of twelve, is quite inaccurate – though every school teacher will know that different years of pupils have quite different group personalities, some with a lot of pupils who are particularly bright, others very slow, others cheerful, others antagonistic. However, as we shall see, the season, the month, the day and the hour of birth also each have their own animal, and the complex interplay of several different animal characteristics – together with the five elements – is what makes up each person's individual personality.

In the ancient Chinese method of interpreting qualities as pairs of opposing but complementary contrasts (Yang and Yin) the symbolic animals in years ending in an even number (Rat, Tiger, Dragon, Horse, Monkey and Dog) are Yang, and those in years ending in an odd number (Ox, Cat, Snake, Sheep, Rooster and Pig) are Yin – very loosely, in Western terms, positive and negative, male and female, deductive and intuitive, hard and soft, thrusting and yielding, penetrating and receiving, etc.

The animals and their characteristics relate to each other in Yang-Yin pairs:

The Rat and Ox both appreciate the value of hard work in a project, the Rat at its conception and birth, the Ox as it grows through to satisfactory completion.

The Tiger and the Cat are the dark and light side of reconciling difficult problems, in an assertive or a conciliatory way.

The Dragon and the Snake both love the mysterious, the Dragon as a showman, the Snake as a mystic.

The Horse and the Sheep epitomize Yang and Yin: the aggressive, masculine Horse and the caring, sensitive Sheep.

The Monkey and the Rooster both achieve career success in an atmosphere of rapid change, the Monkey through versatility and skill, the Rooster through single-mindedness and ambition.

The Dog and the Pig represent the home and family; the Dog is protective, giving security, while the Pig cares for and nurtures the family.

A b o v e : Chinese astrology shares much of its imagery, symbolism and even meaning with the astrology of other Eastern and Oriental cultures: similar figures, gods, personifications and signs can be found in Persian, Arabic, Indian, and many other systems.

L e f t : This eighteenth-century woodblock print shows the twelve animals of the Chinese zodiacal system around the outer band, and the twelve corresponding character symbols on the inner band.

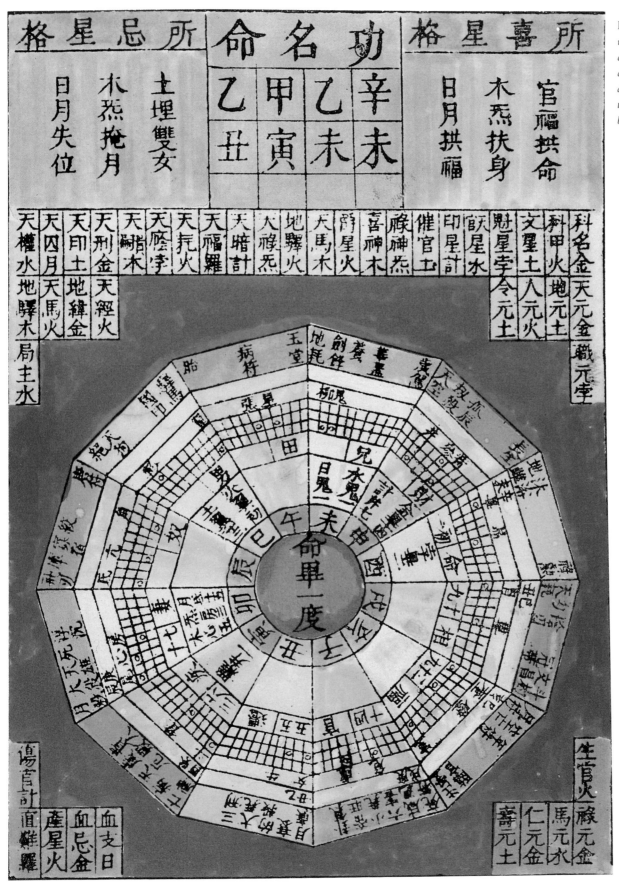

Left: *This hand-coloured woodblock print, which is shown courtesy of a private American collector, illustrates a horoscope diagram with the characters for the twelve animals in the central band.*

Chinese fortune-telling

Chinese fortune-telling stems from Chinese philosophy, at the heart of which is the idea of balance between opposites. Westerners often see Yang and Yin simply as masculine and feminine, but they are far more than this; they include the complementary ideas of positive and negative, active and passive, penetrating and yielding, ruling and submitting, hard and soft, bright and dark, heaven and earth, amongst many others.

The balance between these paired qualities is fundamental to Chinese astrology, the *I Ching*, and the adaptation of the game of Mah Jong for fortune-telling.

Natural phenomena, animals, flowers and different human occupation are seen in these modern Mah Jong cards, designed for use in fortune-telling.

The Animals

Rat

Rats are intelligent, hard-working, assertive and ambitious. Their ambition is of supreme importance; Rats are usually careful with money – sometimes mean – but will spend it to further their career. They are also very generous to the object of their affections. They are friendly and extremely charming, but have a quick temper if they feel their plans – which they keep to themselves – are being threatened. Usually honest, they will lie to protect their career.

Compatible with Dragons and Monkeys.
Problems with Tigers and Dogs.

The Rat Year is a good time to start new plans. Creativity will flourish and artistry come to the fore.
Reorganization. Good for health and romance.

Ox

Ox people are patient, steady, methodical, reliable, solid, sometimes stolid, sometimes stubborn. They are very hard-working, but do not like innovation; the old ways are the best. Tradition and traditional values are important to them; they like order, and can be authoritarian. They are intelligent, but not terribly imaginative. They need security; they can be too materialistic. In love they are slow to get started, but are then steadfast. Compatible with Snakes and Roosters.
Problems with Sheep, other Ox people, Dogs and Tigers.

The Ox Year is a time of stability and steady success. Any new projects should be initiated as soon as possible. A good year for farming.

Tiger

Tigers are born leaders: assertive, sometimes aggressive, very competitive. They are completely self-motivated, and can be selfish. They can easily dazzle others (and subdue them) with their brilliance and their magnetic personalities, but they also have a certain nobility. They are dynamic and enthusiastic, often reckless; they take risks, and can be dangerous to be with, though exciting; they can easily wear others out. In love they are passionate and have a wild streak, but tend to settle down later.

Compatible with Dogs and Horses, perhaps Pigs and Dragons.
Problems with Monkeys, Oxen and Cats.

The Tiger Year is a time of change and turbulence, for good or for bad. Love affairs are passionate, but health can be problematic; accidents can easily happen.

Above: *The Chinese zodiacal images of the Rat and the Ox are carved in relief on a highly-decorated column in the Chinese Garden in Sydney.*

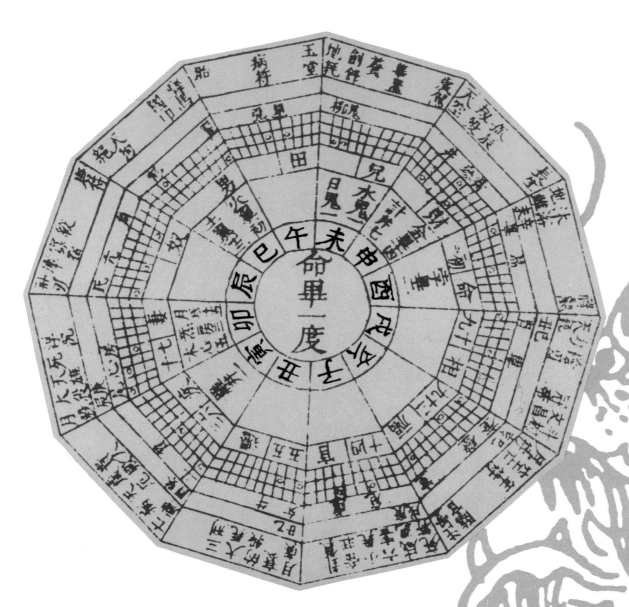

Above: In many respects the Chinese horoscope illustrated here does not look greatly different from the Western horoscopes shown earlier. The inner, black band carries the characters associated with the twelve animals of the Chinese astrological system.

Cat/Rabbit

Cats can be aloof from others; they tend to be quiet, and get on with things by themselves, though in fact they like the security of company and are good to be with, making excellent friends. They are survivors; they prefer sensible compromise to destructive confrontation. They are usually peacemakers, but if they have to fight they have tremendous courage. They are good judges of character; they are also healers. Cats are creative and artistic, but can be moody. In love they will flirt with fun, but are really looking for a warm and comfortable relationship.

Compatible with Pigs, Sheep and often Dogs. Problems with Roosters, Tigers, and often Monkeys and Horses.

The Cat Year is one of quiet progress in agreed

undertakings. Love can lead to procreation; a good time for recuperation in health particularly if there have been problems.

Dragon

Dragons tend to be successful. They are full of enthusiasm, and have the gift of inspiring this in others also. They are intelligent, imaginative, lively and independent; they hate being forced into a routine. They love the exotic and the unusual, including the supernatural; they also love show. They are not always easy to get on with, and can prove dangerous enemies; but they can be very good, supportive and helpful friends, if they are allowed to take the lead. They can easily be arrogant and proud.

Compatible with Rats, Monkeys and other Dragons.
Problems with Dogs especially, and with Horses and Sheep.

The Dragon Year will be unusually creative and innovative, especially in the arts and religion. High-risk projects are likely to succeed, but there will also be risks in love and health.

Snake

Snakes are deep-thinking and wise, but subtle; their success is often because they have manipulated other people, or made good use of their connections. They love finding things out, whether in gossip about other people, or in investigative research – but they are very secretive. They are critical and self-critical; they can be devious, and hold grudges. Like the Dragon, they enjoy mystery, but without the showiness; they are often mystical or psychic. They are often graceful and refined, and love luxury. In love they are sensuous; they will not take second best; they can be very jealous.

Compatible with Roosters and Oxen.
Problems with Pigs, Monkeys, Horses and often Tigers.

The Snake Year can be a time of deviousness and double-dealing, but should be successful if calmness prevails. Avoid potential scandal in relationships.

Right: *A Chinese "Feng Shui" chart from a modern almanac. One important element of Feng Shui is the art and science of fortuitous placement. When siting a new building, for example, the builders will first consult Feng Shui to confirm that the spirits are good and that the area is well-favoured.*

Below: *In Chinese astrology the Horse personality is sociable, competitive, gregarious, fairly solid and stable, healthy and robust. In Horse years consolidation is the watchword rather than excitement.*

Horse

Horses are sociable people, the sort who will belong to social or sports clubs, and take an active part in team sports; they are usually strong and healthy. Horses are not terribly inventive, but enjoy conversation. They are archetypally Yang, and like to be popular, and tend to be self-centred, though not selfish. They are hard-working and make good work-mates, and are naturally gregarious. They are quite well-liked by others, but their behaviour can be unpredictable and they can have nasty tempers. Their hearty exterior often masks an underlying weak and insecure personality. They fall deeply in love, but really they are "in love with love" – or with themselves – and fall out of love just as easily.

Below: *Those who possess a goat personality are kind and considerate, yet can often be over-sensitive. Goat people tend to remain within a crowd rather than rise to a leadership role.*

Compatible with Dogs, Tigers and Sheep.
Problems with Rats, Snakes and Cats.

The Horse Year is one of strength and stability in both the business and the personal world. Health should be sound; any experiences of love will be active rather than deep.

Sheep/Goat

Sheep are vulnerable rather than insecure. They are archetypally Yin: good, gentle, considerate people, very caring, who make good listeners and offer a shoulder to cry on; but because they know how very easily they can be wounded they do not always reveal themselves fully to others. They react badly to criticism, always taking it personally; they can easily become depressed. They are diplomatic, and avoid confrontation. They are

artistic, though not creative in the sense of originality. They can appear vague and tend to be dreamers. In relationships they are more compatible with people who are tougher and less sensitive than themselves.

Compatible with Pigs, Cats, Horses – and other Sheep.
Problems with Oxen, Rats, Monkeys, Roosters.

The Sheep Year is one of peace, diplomacy and humanitarianism. The Arts are well-favoured; so is love.

Monkey

Monkeys can beguile anyone with their charm. They are clever, quick-witted and resourceful, but can be devious, deceitful and unscrupulous. They tend to be amoral rather than actively immoral: they are natural tricksters. They are fast learners, highly inventive, and extremely good at problem-solving. They thrive in an atmosphere of change. They are always able to get out of an awkward situation by quick thinking, and often by their innate humour. They are vivacious and friendly to everyone, which can be irritating for a new partner – and they are likely to change partners frequently. They are intelligent, but they tend to be vain, holding a low opinion of most other people. Overall, Monkeys are highly complex people.

Compatible with other Monkeys, Rats and Dragons.
Problems with Tigers and Snakes.

The Monkey Year is one of change, instability and confusion in business, love and health; it should be approached with care.

Rooster

Roosters often come over as abrasive, sometimes aggressive, throwing all their attention and energies into whatever they are pursuing, and ignoring or forgetting everything and everybody else. They are intelligent and intensely ambitious, and suffer fools badly; but they are very efficient, and good organizers. Like Monkeys they love variety and change, and thrive on activity. They can be great fun to be with if you can stand the pace – and

Bottom, right: The basic attributes of the Rooster personality are self-confidence, determination and pride. These can easily slip over into arrogance and aggression. Roosters are shrewd, well-organized and love a challenge.

Below: A charming domino card from The Story of the River's Bank *set.*

white, and they are born worriers. They tend to be suspicious of others and their motives until they get to know them. This can make it very difficult at the start of a relationship but once trust has been established, Dog people will be utterly loyal; they are natural home-makers and protectors. They do not, however, like public displays of emotion.

Compatible with Horses and Tigers.
Problems with Dragons, Roosters and Sheep.

The Dog Year is a time to think of defence, whether of the country, the business or the home. Health will be strong; love will be faithful.

Pig

Pig people are caring and loving people who work hard for the good of their family; they make excellent husbands, wives and parents. They are honest, sincere and tolerant, and expect others to be the same, which means that others can easily take advantage of them; in some ways they can be very naïve. Because they put their family before everything else they are unlikely to rise to the top of their professions; many of them work in "caring careers" where personal ambition is less important than the work they accomplish. They are also very practical people, who never leave jobs unfinished. They sometimes hide a warm heart under a bluff exterior, but anyone who knows them will quickly see beneath the apparent roughness, which, at times, can even appear to be rudeness. In love they are earthy and sensual.

Compatible with Cats and Dogs.
Problems with Snakes and Monkeys.

The Pig Year should be devoted to the welfare of the family; it is also a time of rest and reflection, and of drawing projects to a most satisfactory conclusion.

Far left: The Monkey is one of the most charming and seductive of the twelve animal characters. Perhaps best summarized in Western terms as a "lovable rogue", the Monkey is sharp, witty, streetwise, flexible, and ambitious. Its energy can also get it into trouble, however: it overstretches, takes risks, and ignores the rules.

they are basically honest and straightforward, which is why they sometimes appear to be rude and tactless. They like to be the centre of attention, often performing to the gallery; they can be downright eccentric. In love, Roosters are all or nothing.

Compatible especially with Snakes, and also Oxen and Dragons.
Problems with Cats, Dogs, Monkeys and other Roosters.

The Rooster Year is one of determination, almost to the point of extremism. Business and career are in; love is out. All opinions will be voiced loud and clear.

Dog

Dog people are friendly, honest and likeable, and are steady and hard workers – but they are known for their occasionally sharp tongue. They are fairminded, and have an exaggerated sense of fair play. They are very loyal, and will take the side of friends they feel have been wronged. But they do tend to see things in strict terms of black and

The five elements

Each year also has an element associated with it, and the Chinese have five elements, not the four of the Western world: wood, fire, earth, metal and water. Each element lasts for two years at a time, first exhibiting Yang characteristics, then Yin;

each element therefore covers a Yang-Yin pair of animals, a different element every twelve years. The combination of the animal and the element of each year, a twelve year cycle and a ten year cycle of pairs, offers sixty variants just for the year.

The same sixty possibilities are also available for the season, the month, the date and the time of birth. With this level of complexity, the Chinese horoscope is every bit as rich and detailed as its Western equivalent. The Chinese astrologer looking for the most propitious time for a new enterprise has a very wide spread of information.

The five elements affect the nature of the symbolic animal. To take the Snake as an example, it appears that the Wood-Snake is more considerate of others' feelings, the Fire-Snake is more suspicious and power-hungry, the Earth-Snake is more slow-minded and likeable and the Metal-Snake is both more secretive and more logical, while the Water-Snake is more artistic but more jealous – all these in addition to the basic Snake type.

The elements also relate to each other. Depending on the combination and positioning of the elements at different periods of someone's life in their chart, they have a tremendous effect on the personality, the directions one takes, and the relative success of different endeavours.

Wood burns, giving fire
Fire leaves ash or earth
Earth contains metal
Metal when heated flows like water
Water gives life to wood

Any adjacent pair of these has an overall good effect. But the elements can also go together in another order, and an adjacent pair of these would be destructive.

Wood sucks the goodness out of earth
Earth muddies water
Water quenches fire
Fire melts metal
Metal chops wood

In general, these are the characteristics of each element:

Wood is creative and inspirational, and denotes health and happiness.
Fire is energy and excitement, but can be dangerous.
Earth is connected with stability and the land.
Metal denotes business efficiency – or strife.
Water shows change, intelligence, travel and communications.

Wood years end in 4 or 5 (plus, of course, the beginning of the following year), fire years end in 6 or 7, earth years in 8 or 9, metal years in 0 or 1, and water years in 2 or 3.

Wood	Fire	Earth	Metal	Water	
1934	1936	1938	1940	1942	Yang
1935	1937	1939	1941	1943	Yin
1944	1946	1948	1950	1952	Yang
1945	1947	1949	1951	1953	Yin
1954	1956	1958	1960	1962	Yang
1955	1957	1959	1961	1963	Yin
1964	1966	1968	1970	1972	Yang
1965	1967	1969	1971	1973	Yin
1974	1976	1978	1980	1982	Yang
1975	1977	1979	1981	1983	Yin
1984	1986	1988	1990	1992	Yang
1985	1987	1989	1991	1993	Yin
1994	1996	1998	2000	2002	Yang

Your other self

Many people find that they have two distinct personalities inside them; some people regularly have arguments with themselves. Perhaps they have elements of patience and irritability, or of caring and coldness, or they have conflicting urges to be impetuous or cautious. The theory behind Chinese astrology says that this is because the time of day at which they were born also has the characteristics of one of the symbolic animals; a similar idea, though for different reasons, to the Ascendant in Western astrology. Unlike Western astrology, though, the longitude is irrelevant – 2 a.m. is Ox wherever a person is born in the world – though local time adjustments such as British Summer Time or Daylight Saving Time should certainly be taken into account.

The animal of the time of birth could be called the other self, a companion, conscience or, at times, the darker side of the character.

Tiger, the equivalent tail end of February in the month of the Cat, and so on; if the New Year is in early February, then the month of the Tiger will extend into March, and this continues throughout the year.

There is a further complication in that each animal month may be the same or a day or two shorter than the equivalent calendar month, so that there is likely to be about a ten-day difference by the end of the year; here it is wise to work back from the next Chinese New Year.

Birth time	Other Self
11 p.m. – 1 a.m.	Rat
1 a.m. – 3 a.m.	Ox
3 a.m. – 5 a.m.	Tiger
5 a.m. – 7 a.m.	Cat/Rabbit
7 a.m. – 9 a.m.	Dragon
9 a.m. – 11 a.m.	Snake
11 a.m. – 1 p.m.	Horse
1 p.m. – 3 p.m.	Sheep/Goat
3 p.m. – 5 p.m.	Monkey
5 p.m. – 7 p.m.	Rooster
7 p.m. – 9 p.m.	Dog
9 p.m. – 11 p.m.	Pig

February	Tiger
March	Cat
April	Dragon
May	Snake
June	Horse
July	Sheep
August	Monkey
September	Rooster
October	Dog
November	Pig
December	Rat
January	Ox

Below: *The Chinese call their astrological system "Ming Shui" – the reckoning of Fate. At every significant event – birth, marriage, and death – it plays its role. It is an ancient and revered philosophy, which plays a part in every aspect of the Chinese way of life.*

The month

Each month also relates to one of the symbolic animals, though it is not possible to equate them with the Western star signs because of the variable calendar already mentioned. It is made even more complicated by the fact that, to get the lunar year synchronized with the seasons of the solar year, seven times every nineteen years the Chinese "stretch" one of the months to double its length.

Very roughly, though, the following chart gives an idea of the relationship between the animal signs and the Western calendar months. If the date of the New Year is in January, then the tail end of January is included in the month of the

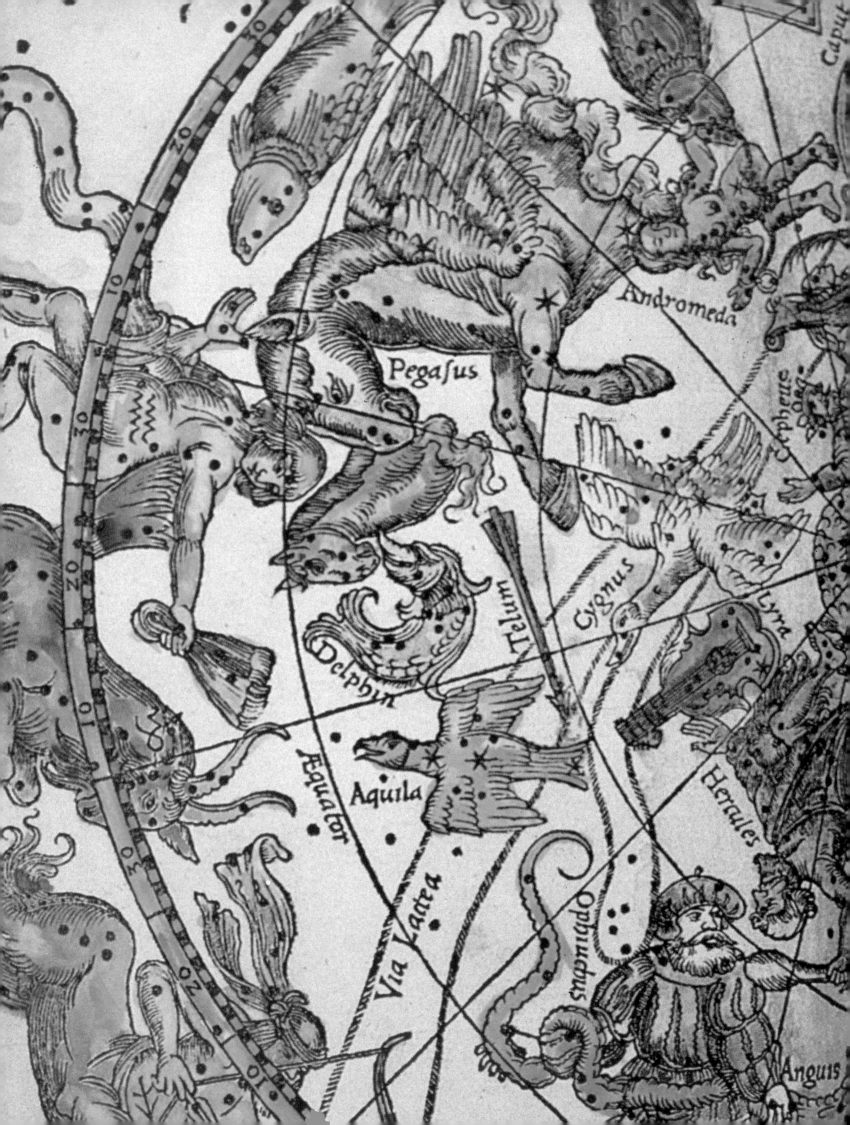

Personal Systems

*M*any systems of divination and prediction are concerned with the interpretation or manipulation of outside elements – Tarot cards, rune stones, I Ching stalks amongst them – but one of the finest mediums for divination is much closer to home: your own body.

Nothing is truer or more difficult to disguise than your physical attributes. The shape of the head, the features, the lines on the hand, and the way you write (even when you are attempting to conceal your identity) can all, to an experienced observer and interpreter, provide inescapable clues to the inner thoughts, the personality, and, through this knowledge, to likely future events in your life.

Phrenology and physiognomy, which were massively popular in the nineteenth century, today have a smaller following: but graphology is more credible than ever before as a revealer of character traits, and palm-reading will always be the most cherished and revered of divinatory skills.

Opposite: *Phrenology was never an exact science, with one agreed codification of attributes always associated with the same area of the cranium. As in many divinatory systems, different schools and theories grew out of the same basic idea. This image illustrates a system using 40 classifications.*

Palmistry

The traditional image of a palm reader is of a raven-haired gypsy woman at a fair whose palm is crossed with silver as payment for revealing the secrets that she sees in her customers' hands. Part of this mystery still remains today, preserved through the art of both chiromancy, reading the future in the hand, and chirognomy, reading one's character in the hand.

Below: In the medieval period, divinatory systems were intermingled rather than clearly separated mediums. This 1533 plate from Agrippa's De Occulta Philosophia illustrates a system combining palmistry and astrology.

Careful hand analysts will today look at far more than the lines on the palm of the hand; they will also examine the knuckles and the back of the hand, the shape of the finger-nails, the length of the fingers compared to the palm, the relative size and angle of the thumb, and even the colouring and texture of the skin. Both hands should be examined rather than just one.

Above: This medieval zodiacal man illustrates the way that esoteric scholars of the time viewed the body. The theory was that each part of the anatomy was governed by external forces ruled by one of the astrological signs, thus linking individual physical properties with fate, destiny, and the cosmic forces.

As in the case of, for example, dreams, astrology, Tarot, and, in fact, any form of prediction or divination, the lines on your hand (and all the other factors) do not predict a fixed future; they tell you more about yourself, and thus reveal potentialities. Chiromancy is unlikely to tell you that you will definitely be married twice and have three sons and a daughter (though some palmists are remarkably accurate in such predictions); but it can tell you that you are likely to be a stable, loyal, loving partner, or that you are the sort of person who will rush headlong into relationships, or that you will be very close to children. It will not tell you that you will come into a fortune when you are thirty-five but it might tell you that you have a sound business sense, and should pursue (or avoid) certain career paths.

Similarly, to dispel a common myth, the length of the life line does *not* tell you how long you are going to live; but the line can give some indication of the strength of your life, especially your health. Again, the lines will not say that you will break your leg when you are forty; but certain things about them might point out childhood illnesses, and can (along with other factors) give an indication that you might have something wrong with your digestion or your breathing or your nerves.

Interestingly, such signs of illness in the lines will fade away once the illness is cured. One example is the presence of many thin vertical lines down the fingers, showing that someone is under a lot of stress. When the stress is lifted the skin on the palm side of the fingers may become smoother.

Health warning

Although a small number of Western doctors are beginning to take certain aspects of chiromancy seriously (as doctors in the past – and in the East – always have done), and to use hand analysis to detect the potential for certain illnesses, your own hand is not a diagnostic map for you to depend on yourself. If you think you detect signs of a particular medical complaint in your own hand or in anyone else's, consult a medical doctor. It is not your job to diagnose illnesses through esoteric or alternative means. All forms of divination should only be used for good – and occasionally the best good you can do is to persuade your friend or client to go to a doctor, without worrying them. Do not play doctor yourself.

A b o v e : *The great German chiromancer Johann Hartlieb, author of the earliest printed book on palmistry* Die Kunst Ciromantia, *which was published in 1475.*

O v e r : *Pietro della Vecchia's seventeenth-century painting, Il Chiromante, shows a nobleman having his future told by a palm-reader.*

Aspects of the Hand

Above: *Chiromancy (palm-reading) has been a respected method of recognizing and interpreting aspects of the character and personality for hundreds of years.*

The lines on your right and left hand will probably be fairly similar, but they will not be identical. Palm readers say this is because the dominant or active hand (the right hand for right-handed people, the left for left-handed) shows our living character, i.e. what we are actually making of what we were given to start off with – which is what is shown in the passive hand (the left for right-handed people, the right for left-handed). Another way of looking at it is that the dominant hand shows how we present ourselves in the world, while the passive shows how we really are inside.

It is essential to read both hands, and to note the differences between them. These can show, for example, a triumph of will over unpromising attributes, or a lack of development of potential abilities. They can also reveal internal personality conflicts, which is where skilled hand-analysts can find themselves (rightly or wrongly) taking on the role of a psychotherapist.

Above: *This hand-coloured woodblock plate appeared in Hartlieb's* Die Kunst Ciromantia – *the first ever chiromantic publication.*

~ 73 ~

Right: *In the seventeenth and eighteenth centuries, many aristocrats and influential people had themselves painted in the process of having their palms read: an ironic pose, considering that this is conceivably the only time a lady such as this would have ever come into such direct physical contact with a person of another class or background. Prediction is a great equalizer.*

Shape of the hand

There are two common nineteenth century ways of dividing up hand shapes. Casimir d'Arpentigny, a nineteenth-century French palm reader found seven hand shapes: elementary, square, spatulate, philosophic, conic, psychic and mixed. The brilliant palm reader (and charlatan) Louis Hamon, known as Cheiro, used this method, which accounts for its continuing popularity. The German Carl Carus preferred four divisions: elementary, motoric, sensitive and psychic. Another method used eight divisions: the Earth and the seven traditional astrological planets.

Perhaps the most straightforward is the modern esoteric authority Fred Gettings' four-fold elemental division, based on the length and breadth of the palm, and the relative length of the fingers; the fingers are said to be long if the middle finger from its tip to its join with the palm is three-quarters (or more) the length from the join to the top rascette, or bracelet on the wrist.

The Earth hand has a square palm and short fingers; these people are earthy, practical, sensible,

blunt and sometimes gloomy. The air hand has a square palm and long fingers; air people are intellectual rather than emotional, inquisitive, and good communicators, but can be cold. Fire hands have oblong palms and short fingers; their owners are active, energetic, extrovert, impulsive, and prone to flashes of fiery temper. Water hands have oblong palms and long fingers; water people are sensitive, emotional, caring, understanding, but easily led and easily wounded.

In all mentions of size, it is relative size that counts, rather than physical size. In general, small people have small hands, and large people have large hands; women's hands are usually smaller and less chunky than men's; children's are obviously smaller than adults'. But if a woman is sturdy and square-framed, she will probably have large, "masculine" hands; if a man is slender and fine-boned, his hands may look more "feminine". If you meet exceptions to these general rules, examine the hands carefully to see what more they can tell you.

The mounts

These are significant on two counts: how well-developed they are (rounded or flat, firm or puffy), and which lines run into them. Size is not everything; over-development is as significant as under-development.

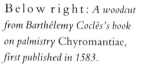

Below right: *A woodcut from Barthélemy Coclès's book on palmistry* Chyromantiae, *first published in 1583.*

At the base of the palm:
The Mount of Venus is the fleshy part of the palm at the base of the thumb. This rules, as might be expected, warmth, love and sex.
The Mount of Luna (or the Moon) is on the opposite side of the palm, by the percussive edge of the hand (the edge you would use to chop or strike something). This signifies imagination and creativity, and a romantic nature.
The Mount of Neptune lies between these two; those palm readers who use it say it signifies a strong, charismatic personality.

At the top of the palm:
The Mount of Jupiter is at the base of the index finger; it signifies power, good fortune and leadership.
The Mount of Saturn is at the base of the middle finger; it shows a quiet, prudent, thoughtful,

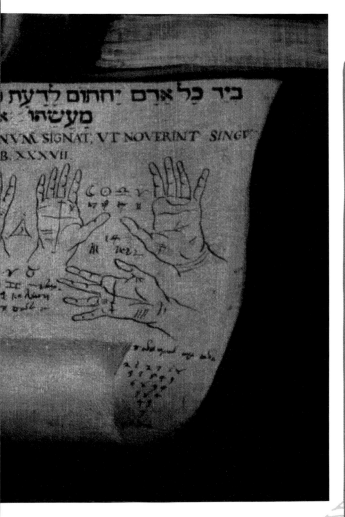

balanced .person, probably studious, possibly mystical.

The Mount of Apollo (or the Sun) is at the base of the ring finger; it signifies aesthetic appreciation, of both art and beauty, and also a happy personality.

The Mount of Mercury is at the base of the little finger; it shows liveliness and wit, versatility, and verbal communication.

In the middle:

The middle third of the hand is ruled by Mars. In the space between the base of the index finger and the inside base of the thumb, the Mount of Mars active (or positive) shows strength and courage, ranging from aggression to cowardice.

Opposite that, on the percussive side of the palm, the Mount of Mars passive (or negative) shows passive courage, the moral virtue rather than the physical strength.

Between these lies the Plain of Mars, the hollow of the palm, which shows capability and practicality if well-developed.

A b o v e : *An illustration showing the meanings of signs found upon the palm of the hand and their influence on the individual. This is the first page of Hartlieb's famous* Die Kunst Ciromantia.

The Fingers and Thumb

Each finger relates to one of the gods (rather than planets), as in their mounts except for Apollo whose characteristics are similar to those of the Sun. Apollo is also traditionally linked with medicine and music.

The length of each finger, and the length and prominence of each phalange or joint in relation to the others, indicates the presence and strength of each personality trait. Remember that it is as significant for a trait to be over-developed as under-developed. The first phalange (the joint with the nail) denotes mental characteristics and intuition, the middle practical, financial and business qualities, and the third material, earthy and sensual aspects. If any phalange is disproportionately long or short, it is likely to be a bad rather than a good sign.

A strong index (Jupiter) finger, then, would show strength of character and leadership qualities. If markedly long, it shows a domineering, arrogant personality; if markedly short, a reluctance to take responsibility.

A strong middle (Saturn) finger is likely to denote a serious, introspective, perhaps scientific character; if very long it shows coldness and a gloomy personality, if very short, flippancy and irresponsibility.

A strong ring (Apollo) finger shows emotional stability and artistic talent; if the finger is very long, vanity and a tendency to gamble, if very short, timidity, lack of creativity, and an inability to cope with money.

A strong little (Mercury) finger shows a powerful intellect and ability with words; very long implies a loud, garrulous, possibly dishonest person; very short shows a difficulty in expressing ideas in words. Because the little finger is often set much lower down the hand than the others, it is much more important to judge its length rather than where its tip lies against the ring finger. A little finger that has a natural tendency to lie away from the ring finger shows individuality; one that hugs the ring finger shows conventionality and dependancy on others.

The thumb is, literally and figuratively, out on its own. A strong, well-balanced thumb can offset defects revealed by other digits, and reinforce their positive points; a weak thumb weakens

the whole hand. The first phalange represents will-power, the second the reasoning powers; the sensual Mount of Venus can sometimes be thought of as the third phalange. A well-balanced thumb lies between 45 and 90 degrees away from the index finger; closer than that shows someone who is tight-fisted, nervous or narrow-minded; wider shows extravagance, over-generosity and recklessness. A very large, bulbous first phalange, especially with a wide but very short nail, can denote a violent temper; it used to be called "the murderer's thumb".

Above and opposite: *Chinese diagrams showing the locations of the "palaces" of the hand in Chinese palmistry, marked with the eight trigrams of the* I Ching *system.*

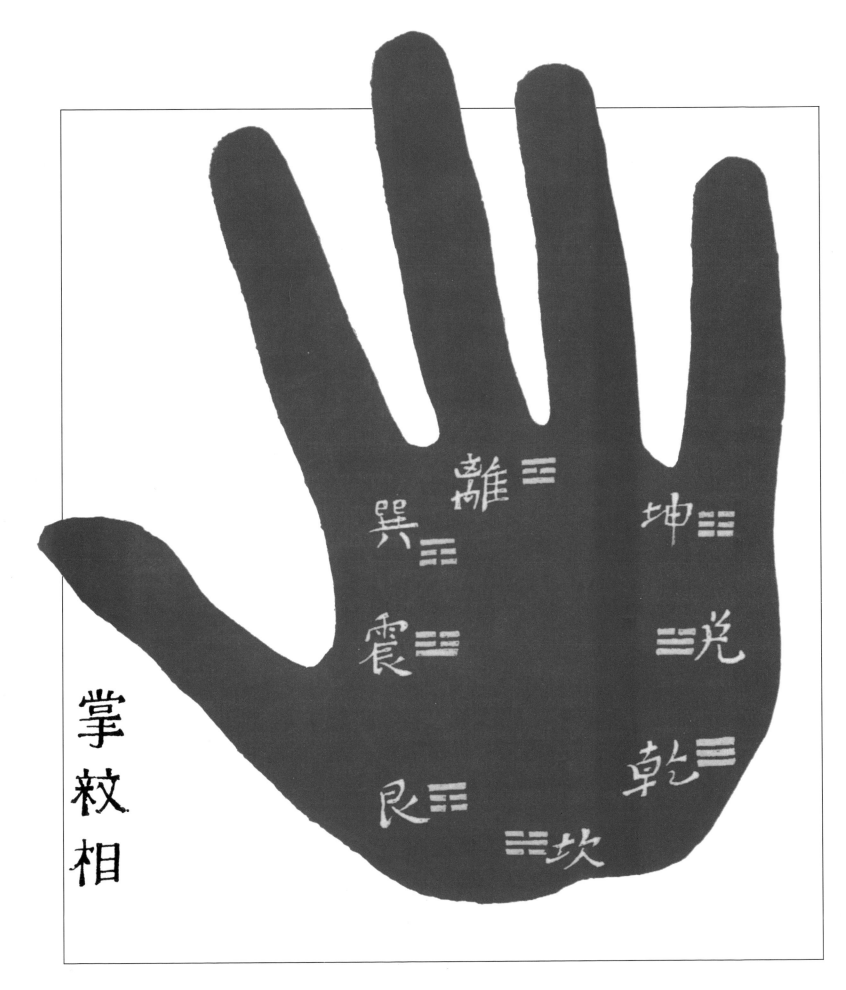

掌紋相

T h e   L i n e s

*P*hysiologically, the lines in the palm are simply where the skin folds and creases when we flex our hands, just as the tiny horizontal lines on the backs of our fingers, and the much more obvious wrinkles on our knuckles, are expansion creases. Skin is very flexible, but such creases, like the pleats of a skirt or the bellows of a concertina, enable it to adjust to a variety of stretching and contracting movements.

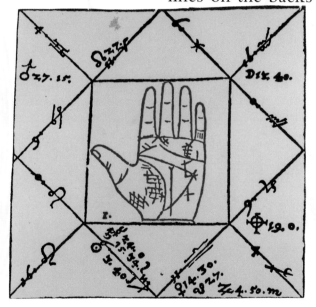

A b o v e : *A print combining symbolism from palmistry and astrology, thus relating the hand to the horoscope. The horoscope itself was cast for 17 August 1567.*

The basic pattern of lines will remain much the same throughout one's life, but individual lines will deepen or fade, lengthen or shorten, develop breaks, spurs, dots or stars. We have seen that the lines can be a very good health indicator; they can also develop as we become more or less assertive or compassionate, for example. Our characters change throughout our lives, and our hands reflect our characters.

Not everybody has all the minor lines, and in some people even some of the major lines are faint or absent; palm readers must work with what they are

Opposite above: *The renowned palmist Barthélemy Coclès doing a reading for a client. This is an illustration from his own sixteenth-century chiromantic text.*

Opposite below: *Gypsies have always been associated with palmistry. Because of their life of perpetual travel, which in olden times was even more wide-ranging (encompassing the whole of Europe and the Middle East), they were rumoured to have acquired and mastered the esoteric mysteries of the world. This is a typically stylized eighteenth-century painting.*

given. We will only deal with the five major lines here in this book.

The Life Line

This is the easiest to find and, in many people, one of the deepest. It is the curved line around the Mount of Venus, or, in more prosaic terms, the crease around the ball of the thumb. This starts at the edge of the hand, between the base of the index finger and the inside base of the thumb, and works down towards the wrist. Generally, the wider the swing of the curve into the palm, the better; it shows an open, generous, outgoing person, while a tight curve shows a more closed-in sort of personality.

The life line does *not* show how long you are going to live; a short life line or one that is broken does *not* mean you are going to die early. This is a popular misconception which should be discounted immediately.

What the life line does show is the strength or intensity of life, both in general health and in major and dramatic changes in one's life. It is quite common for a life line to break and restart, either with or without an overlapping section; this could indicate a major health problem, or a complete change in the way of life. A good, deep, strong line without any chains, islands, crossbars or breaks denotes rude health throughout one's life. Generally, islands and chains show health problems, and crossbars emotional upheavals.

The Heart Line

This is the higher of the two roughly horizontal lines, and runs from the percussive edge of the hand in the general direction of the index finger. The heart line is the indicator of emotional characteristics, particularly in regard to relationships; it is also supposed to show potential physical heart problems, though it must be stressed again that playing the amateur doctor is not a sensible game. Only if negative indicators in the heart line are supported by similar indicators throughout the hand (including the nails) should there be any worry at all, and then the best thing to do is to ask your doctor for a check-up. Self-diagnosis is like the person who reads a family health book from cover to cover and becomes convinced they have eighteen different diseases.

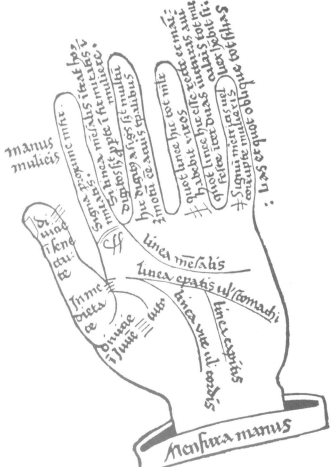

The ideal heart line starts cleanly at the edge of the palm and progresses without any fading, breaks or crossbars, in a smooth curve, to end up near the index finger. This is a warm, loving, dependable, emotionally well-rounded person without any major hang-ups. Few of us are that lucky. A fairly straight line shows that the heart is ruled by the head; "logical lovers" may be clear about how they feel, but their partners tend to find them infuriating. A weak, faded line denotes emotional insecurity. Chaining shows a tendency to fickleness and infidelity. Breaks are supposed to show a broken heart; but the line usually restarts before too long! Forks at the end can be good or bad, depending on where they go: the mounds of Jupiter and Saturn indicate strength and leadership, and deep-thinking (or moodiness) respectively; a fork joining the head line means conflict between the heart and the head, emotion and reason, which is usually bad news.

A b o v e : The four coloured illustrations on these pages are examples of readings by the sixteenth-century palm reader Barthélemy Coclès. They were first published in his book Chyromantiae.

The Head Line

This is the lower of the two horizontal lines, and starts near to, or often joined to the life line,

working its way over to the percussive edge. Along with the thumb, the head line gives the strongest indication of the mind and the will. Generally, the straighter it is, the more analytical the mind; straight head lines are often found on practical, square hands. If it curves down towards the Mount of Luna on the lower percussive edge it shows a more intuitive and imaginative approach. If it starts well above the life line it shows independence, even recklessness; if below it shows nervousness and timidity. If it is joined to the life line, an early separation is fine; but a late separation means a late developer.

Forks show diversity, but can bring confusion. A fork up to, or starting beneath the middle finger is associated with intense study, a fork under the ring finger with writing talent, and a fork under the little finger with business success.

The Simian Line

There is a rare case where the heart and head lines are one line, a horizontal slash across the palm known as the Simian line. It usually denotes someone with extreme intensity, of concentration

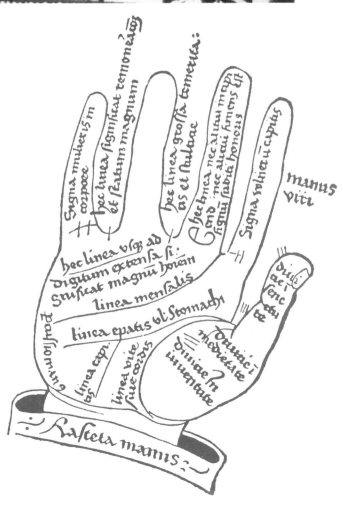

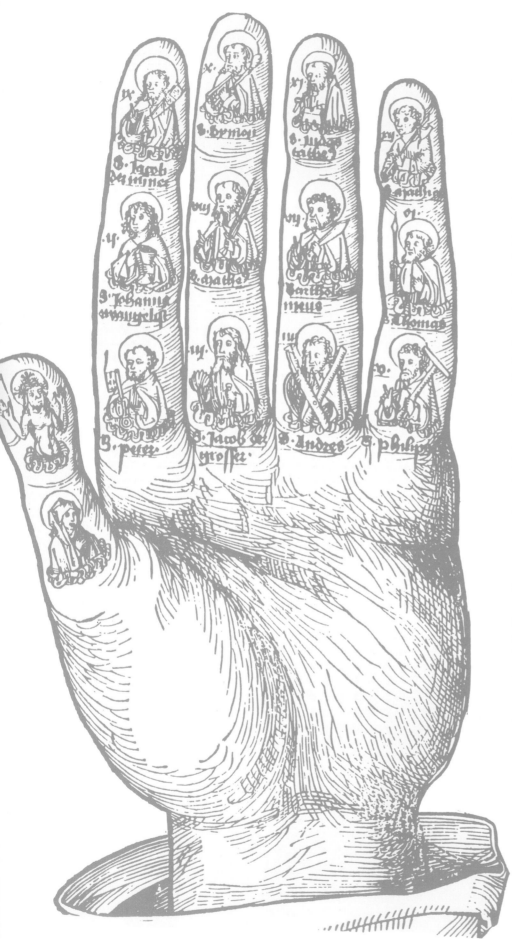

or emotion or purpose, who works with single-minded devotion for what they want. They love and hate and believe absolutely, with no room for doubt; everything is either black or white.

The Fate Line

This is a vertical line, usually starting at or near the wrist and going up through the middle of the palm to end near the base of the fingers. It is sometimes called the Line of Saturn, though the chances are that it will not reach that far, or that it ends somewhere else. It can also be called the destiny line.

Despite its name this line does not predict one's fate. Although more than any other line it is supposed to indicate success or failure in life, what it really shows is the effect of external influences on our lives – and this, as always, is up to us. Indeed, some palm readers say that a complete absence of the fate line means that we are in full control of our own pattern of living, without any help from anyone else; others say that an absent or very faint fate line shows a happy-go-lucky person, unconcerned with the direction of their life. The fate line, like all lines, must be read in conjunction with the rest of the hand.

The start and end points of the fate line are particularly important. If it starts at the wrist it indicates self-reliance: making your own fate. If it starts from the life line it shows strong family influences, which could be working in and inheriting the family business, or having your life ruled by a domineering parent. Starting from the Mount of Luna shows a changeable, uncertain career, perhaps in the public limelight: the arts, for example. If the fate line starts high up, near the head line, it shows a late start, and perhaps a hard slog before success occurs.

The classic fate line runs up to the Mount of Saturn at the base of the middle finger, showing responsibility and success in a settled, conventional way – a family man with a safe and steady but unexciting job, for example. If it ends on the Mount of Jupiter it shows ambitions and self-motivation, and on the Mount of Apollo creativity and a leaning towards the arts.

The Apollo Line

Known also as the Sun, success, fortune or fame line, this runs parallel to the fate line, closer to the percussive edge of the hand; it is usually shorter, starting higher up the hand, and it ideally runs towards the Apollo or ring finger. This line is often missing from a palm, but this does not mean a complete lack of success; the line is more to do with unusual success.

The fact that it usually starts fairly high up the hand shows that such success or fame should not be expected young, unless it is recognized early on that a person is exceptionally gifted and talented. More usually success and renown are built up as abilities develop through life.

Timing the Lines

This is a highly contentious issue, as there are many different methods of turning palm-lines into time-lines; most of these methods contradict each other and none of them (given the size of the hand as a life-calendar) can be entirely accurate. Line-timing lays a heavier emphasis on foretelling the future (for example "You will have an unhappy love relationship or an abrupt change of job or a serious illness when you are thirty-five or forty-two years old"); this can lead to the popular misconception about a short life line meaning an early death.

Some palm readers determine a mid-life point on each line, and work backwards and forwards; others start at the beginning. As a general rule, given the dimensions of the hand, a millimetre (or $\frac{1}{32}$ in) a year is the accepted measurement. This depends on accurately establishing a base-point, and any miscalculation or blunt pencil will throw it out. The fate and Apollo lines are measured from the bottom upwards, and the life and head lines from the thumb side of the palm towards the percussive side; the heart line used to be measured from thumb side to percussive side as well, but modern palm readers usually say that instead it starts at the percussive edge and progresses towards the index finger.

Some general idea can be given, of whether something is earlier or later in life – but do not forget that lines change through your life, deepening, fading, lengthening, shortening, breaking, forking, growing or losing cross-bars, and so on. The lines change as your life changes.

The future is not fixed in your hands – but your character may well be revealed there.

Mount of Venus

Life Line

Heart Line

Head Line

Health Line

Phrenology and Physiognomy

Phrenology

Phrenology is the art – or science – of judging personality types and traits (and hence divining elements of the subject's future) by way of examining bumps on the head. It was devised – or at least codified – by a doctor, Franz Joseph Gall, who was born near Baden in 1758. He began lecturing on his theories in Vienna around 1796. In brief, the idea of phrenology is that the shape of the skull reveals the shape of the brain beneath it, and that over-developed or under-developed parts of the brain are responsible for character differences. Gall identified thirty-seven different parts of the brain which he called "organs".

He divided the organs into two main sets, affective and intellectual. The affective organs he divided into eleven at the back of the head and over the ear which controlled propensities, or essential qualities, and twelve on the top of the head controlling sentiments or emotions; the intellectual organs were twelve above the nose and eyes to do with perception, and two high on the forehead to

Below: A nineteenth-century phrenology chart showing the main distribution of the areas relating to attitudes, temperaments, and the other characteristics.

Above: An illustration from Jean Belot's 1649 publication Oeuvres *indicating the location of the planetary parts of the human face.*

Right: *A portrait of Dr Franz Joseph Gall (1758– 1828). Many ancient and medieval scholars had dabbled with physiognomical study, but Gall was the first modern academic to attempt to give serious scientific credibility to his discipline.*

do with reason. The Table of Phrenology gives a reference to the thirty-seven affective organs. The brain being made up of two lobes, these thirty-seven organs are repeated on each side.

As in palmistry, if an organ is under-developed, the person may have a deficiency in that particular property; if over-developed, an excess. Number 12, for example, if under-developed would show someone with an inferior-ity complex; if over-developed someone who is arrogant and egotistical. Similarly number 13 shows the range from vanity to a total disregard for what others think. Number 20 ranges from fanatical religious or superstitious belief to utter scepticism about everything to do with the spir-itual or supernatural.

The proportions of different organs or groups of organs is supposed to be able to reveal not only the character but the abilities of the person. Clear-ly someone with 33 and 34 well-developed would make a good musician, while those with 37 make excellent philosophers or politicians.

Modern science has gradually revealed that the whole basis of Gall's theory is fallacious. The brain does not actually touch the inside of the skull at any point, so hillocks and hollows on the head bear no relation to what is inside.

Similarly, the size and shape of the head in fact says little about the brain, and the size of the brain has no proven relationship to the intelligence or ability of its owner.

However, phrenology has been with us for two centuries, and many brilliant men and women have devoted a significant part of their lives to it. Could this be a situation where the right results were achieved by the wrong methods? *Is* there any truth in phrenology? Even if this is in doubt, the experimentation can be entertaining.

Table of Phrenology:

Affective organs

Propensities or Essential Qualities
1 Amativeness: love and sexual energy
2 Self-preservation
3 Parental instincts
4 Inhabitiveness, domesticity
5 Friendship
6 Combativeness, competitiveness
7 Destructiveness, impatience
8 Secretiveness
9 Acquisitiveness
10 Alimentiveness, appetite
11 Constructiveness, achievements

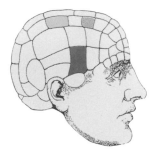

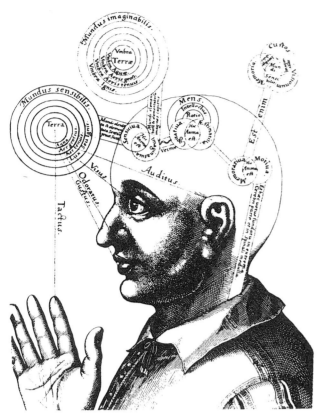

Sentiments or Emotions

12 Self-esteem
13 Approbativeness, desire for approval, vanity
14 Cautiousness, prudence
15 Benevolence
16 Veneration, respect
17 Firmness, determination
18 Conscientiousness
19 Hope, optimism
20 Wonder, belief
21 Ideality, beauty
22 Mirthfulness, humour
23 Imitation, emulation

Intellectual organs

Perception

24 Individuality, perspicacity, observation
25 Form, shape, spacial awareness and memory
26 Size, appreciation of measurement and proportion
27 Weight, physical awareness and balance
28 Colour and tone appreciation
29 Locality, place memory
30 Number, arithmetical ability
31 Order, methodical nature, tidiness
32 Eventuality, memory of events
33 Time sense, chronological perception, rhythm
34 Tune, melody, harmony appreciation and musical ability

35 Language, verbal, oratorical or true linguistic ability

Reason

36 Comparison, analysis, constructive thinking
37 Causality, logical thought

Physiognomy

If the probity of nineteenth century phrenology, as developed by Gall, is in doubt, there may well be clues to the character from the general shape of the head and the distribution of features on it. "I wouldn't trust him, his eyes are too close together." "He's a vicious-looking brute." "You can tell she's artistic just by looking at her." Very often these instant assessments are accurate, a fact that television and film producers make use of in casting actors as characters. "Character" actors often complain that they are being typecast, but there are faces that we can instantly recognize as portraying a villain, an intellectual, or a sultry lover.

It is not always the case, however. "You wouldn't think it to look at him, but he's one of their top scientists." "I know he looks rough, but he's one of the gentlest people you'll ever meet." Those same film producers delight in fooling us by turning the character with the most soft, friendly, unassuming and pleasing face into a cold-blooded murderer.

A b o v e l e f t : *A famous seventeenth-century illustration by Robert Fludd which shows the significance of parts of the head, external and internal influences and supposed mental abilities.*

A b o v e : *In the nineteenth century phrenology experienced an enormous wave of popularity; not just with students of the esoteric, but also with a much wider general public. So voguish was it that it infiltrated every type of social and cultural medium – as illustrated by this magazine cartoon.*

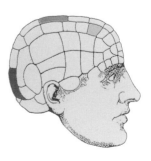

Above: *The title page of the*   *phrenological work,*
famous chiromantic,   Ludiculrum Chriomanticum
physiognomical and   Praetoris.

Having close-set eyes, a receding chin, small, large, high or low ears, a nose of a certain shape and size, prominent cheekbones, a wide mouth, full or thin lips – do these characteristics show character? Or is it more what we do with these physical features rather than the features themselves? With the same features we can look full of hate, angry, serious, sullen, bored, relaxed, pleased, happy, excited, loving. We can spot these signs in other people at a glance. Actors, again, are well trained in this use of their features.

Some people are extremely skilled at reading the more subtle signs of what we now call "body language": a good priest or counsellor, psycho-therapist or doctor, for example – and also fortune-tellers of all kinds. The best palm or Tarot readers, for example, probably pick up just as much, if not more, from their reading of the whole person as from the palm or the cards, and often quite unconsciously.

This is especially helpful when the reader has to make a choice between quite different inter-

The illustrations on these two pages are from early physiognomical works which compared human types with types from the animal world. Facial traits were often compared to animals representative of signs of the zodiac, such as Taurus the bull or Capricorn the goat, as an indication of the corresponding characteristics in people born under a particular sign. However, modern sensitivity to the quite unacceptable racist overtones of the comparison between certain racial types and animals accounts for some of the lessening in popularity and credibility of physiognomy as a fully-fledged science.

pretations of the palm or cards; one feels right, while the others do not seem to apply. Intuition is the most valuable asset for any reader.

One of the major causes of inter-racial distrust and misunderstanding is that we find it more difficult to read the more subtle of these signs in the faces of people of other races.

Interestingly, there is also inter-species misunderstanding. Why do cats always jump on the lap of the one person in the room who actively dislikes cats? For a cat, wide-open, staring eyes mean a challenge, a possible threat; narrowed eyes are a sign of welcome and trust. Although a cat will know the friendliness of people it is familiar with, it will misunderstand a cat-loving stranger's wide-eyed, happy face. But the person who dislikes cats will shrink back, automatically narrowing their eyes; to a cat this may mean "Hello, I want to be friends."

The eyes, in fact, are one of the best things to look for in judging what a person is really thinking and feeling. It is easy enough to fake a convincing smile but it is a lot more difficult to make eyes sparkle with feigned interest and friendliness while wishing not to be bothered by someone. "The eyes are the windows of the soul," wrote Max Beerbohm, misquoting William Blake. If people will not meet your eyes, traditionally this indicates that they may be hiding something, or are ashamed of something. If they stare brazenly they might be a good actor, but you can often detect either a cockiness or a shiftiness that gives the game away. Compare bright, keen eyes with eyes that are dull and lack-lustre. Notice if someone's eyes are watching your own; remember that they are reading you as well, looking for your own signs of nervousness, boredom or rejection – or friendliness, interest and hope.

The art of physiognomy

The ancient Greeks placed a high reliance on physiognomy, the judging of character by the overall shape of (largely) the head. In the sixteenth to nineteenth centuries a number of people, from poets and pastors to anatomists and physiologists, made studies of physical form, and what it can show of the personality. There are several different methods of analysis in physiognomy; here we shall just look at some of the basics.

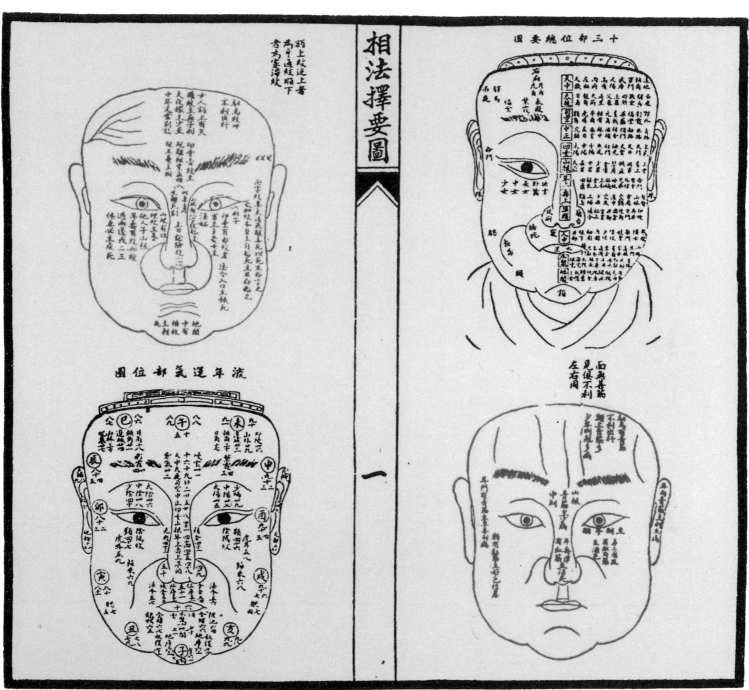

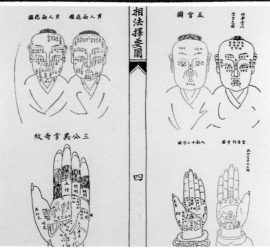

Left : *Animal-human faces surrounding the head of the famous early physiognomical scholar Giovanni della Porta (1538–1615). This illustration was first published in his book* Physiognomia *in 1650.*

Left and above: *The Chinese were interested in physiognomy centuries before any codification of systems was formalized in the West. These illustrations first appeared in "T'ung Shu", an ancient Chinese esoteric almanac.*

It must be pointed out that physiognomy is an old art, and because of its Western origins the majority of studies of physiognomy have been on Caucasians, mainly Western Europeans and white Americans. Because the underlying structure of the head is a different shape for non-Caucasians, whether Chinese, Polynesian, Afro-American, or other racial types, the following cannot be applied as readily to them. As physiognomy has not been widely adopted in current scientific thinking, regrettably no modern studies are available incorporating a contemporary cultural mix of subjects.

The profile is particularly important. The facial angle can be measured against the horizontal by drawing a line from the forehead to the chin, or more generally, the profile can be described as convex, plain or concave.

A convex profile has an outward curve, with the forehead and chin set further back than the nostrils (*not* the tip of the nose); people with this profile are thought to be quick-thinking and quick-tempered. The plane profile, more or less a vertical line, denotes a well-balanced person not given to excesses. The concave profile, with a projecting forehead and chin, shows an unhurried, patient person.

Looking at the front of the face, it can be divided into three sections by drawing a horizontal line at the very top and bottom of the nose. If the three sections are of equal height, the person is well-balanced. If the forehead section is longest, this represents considerable intellectual powers; a long middle section shows a practical, energetic, active person, while a long mouth and chin section denotes determination.

The forehead can be high or low, and narrow or broad. High again indicates intelligence, if narrow the person is good at learning; if broad, it shows inventiveness and creativity. A person with a low forehead is thought to be less intellectual; if narrow it indicates a somewhat dull, conservative narrow-minded personality; if broad it represents a constructive and persevering determination.

Large ears are supposed to show a vibrant, active person; medium-sized ears indicate someone who is open-minded and fair, and small ears someone who is cautious and conservative. If the ears lie flat against the head the person is cautious; if they are projecting the person has more verve.

A protruding chin denotes stubbornness, a receding chin weakness and lack of determination; these can be countered by a broad chin showing strength and conscientiousness, or a narrow chin showing fragility and lack of will power.

Similar theories can be applied to the nose, the eyebrows, the eyes, the cheeks, the mouth and the lips. Some physiognomists also consider the colour of the eyes and hair. Although it can be said that these, like other physical characteristics, are inherited factors, it can also be argued that character and temperament are also partly inherited. Brown eyes traditionally show someone with depth of emotion, both good and bad, and also given to spells of moodiness; blue eyes show self-control and practicality, but also coolness of emotion; green eyes show great intelligence and intensity of emotions, particularly the legendary wild love, artistic nature and fiery temper of the green-eyed redhead.

How much can be read into such "analysis" is open to debate. We all know people whose personality fits in exactly with the small selection of physical attributes discussed here – but we also probably know people who run counter to some or all of these "rules". A physiognomist would say that this is because we are ignoring all sorts of other characteristics. One system uses a table of

Right: These six "types" come from J K Lavater's eighteenth-century book Physiognomical Fragments. *Belying its title, this is one of the most ambitious works on the subject ever produced, as Lavater struggled to create a definitive and comprehensive codification of his discipline.*

sixty pairs of attributes such as boldness and timidity, industry and laziness, modesty and shamelessness, self-indulgence and ascetisism. Each aspect of the appearance – drooping eyelids, high cheekbones, pointed ears – is given anything from three or four up to over a dozen of these attributes, whether positive, average or negative. All the marks for each attribute are then totalled, giving an extremely detailed personality picture.

But the best guide is often simply the gut reaction: "I think I like this person; they seem to be strong-willed without being domineering, and kindly without being cloying," or, "I'm not sure I trust this person; there's something about them that doesn't ring true." Often it is possible to get a pretty good impression before they even begin to speak; whether you call it physiognomy or body language, it is instinctive, and very often surprisingly accurate.

Top and above: *Pre-eighteenth-century physiognomical texts were of a quaint and general nature. Even in Barthélemy Coclès's* Physiognomonia, *commentaries tended towards personal subjective comment rather than objective investigation.*

Right: *This illustration comes from Richard Saunder's book* Physiognomie, Chiromancie, and Metoposcopy, *which was published in 1653. Metoposcopy is the science of relating the positioning and occurence of moles on the body to attributes and personal characteristics. It is little practised today.*

Graphology

Handwriting analysts are very quick to point out that there is nothing occult or esoteric about their work. Graphology is a rational, scientific method of analysing people's characters, they say, and should not be put together with such things as astrology and palmistry.

For those who give some time to things like astrology and/or palmistry, for example, there is no problem: handwriting analysis is just one more way of examining someone's character. Handwriting has been studied for thousands of years. Aesop, Aristotle, Virgil and Julius Caesar all saw merit in examining it; the Roman historian Suetonius, in his biographies of the emperors, always described their writing style. Shakespeare, Sir Walter Scott, Robert Browning and Benjamin Disraeli, amongst many others, practised graphology in one way or another.

In the last few decades, handwriting analysis has become more and more widespread for the two

A b o v e : *Runes were one of the earliest of writing systems; consisting of combinations of straight lines, they were used extensively by the early Norsemen whose literature is today the subject of philological research. In modern times, runes have taken on a more esoteric meaning and are believed to have predictive powers.*

Left: *An impressive marble statue of the great playwright and poet, William Shakespeare. He wrote in an age when there was no set style of English; consequently he was able to experience great freedom of expression while at the same time acting as a strong influence on his readers and audiences. He says in* Henry IV, Part 1: *"I once did hold it, as our statists do,/A baseness to write fair, and laboured much/How to forget that learning; but, sir, now/It did me yeoman's service."*

Right: *A satirical eighteenth-century portrait of an astrologer, Partridge, with his chart as symbolic of superstitious belief. Opposite stands the satirist, Swift (here called Bickerstaff) who represents logic as portrayed through handwriting.*

main purposes of screening job applicants and detecting forgeries.

In the first case, it is more widely used in the USA and continental Europe (especially in Germany and the Netherlands) than in the UK; people are often asked to write their letter of application by hand rather than use a typewriter or word processor. Clearly undesirable character traits revealed by analysis – unreliability, carelessness, untidiness – will cause rejection without even an interview, while for shortlisted applicants, a more detailed analysis will give the interviewers a lot of useful information about the applicant.

Graphologists claim that they can spot whether someone has a critical mind, shows informed judgement, has mental agility, a methodical approach to work, perseverance, or reliability, or if they have confused ideas, or show traces of dishonesty, stubbornness, rigidity of thought, nervousness, evasiveness, egocentricity, hypocrisy, or any mental or emotional imbalance.

In the second case, that of detecting forgery by comparing a questionable piece of writing with known examples, graphologists can prove that a letter, suicide note, will or signature was or was not written by a specific individual. They are also able to point out if the writer's state of mind was seriously disturbed at the time of writing.

It is supposed to be impossible for even an

expert forger to fool an expert graphologist – or a well-programmed computer. Computer analysis of signatures has advanced to such a degree that before long banks are likely to have verification machines on their counters, to compare a customer's on-the-spot signature with that on a credit card, or in the bank's own records.

There is no doubt that graphology works – but how is it done? Different graphologists may concentrate on different areas, but all of them look at the overall impression given by a page of writing before they focus in on any individual characteristics.

The page as a whole

Before looking at the handwriting itself, and the formation of individual letters, the graphologist stands back and looks at the whole page. The way that the writing is arranged on the page gives important information in itself.

The first things to look at are the margins, the slope, the size, the movement, the tension and the pressure of the writing. Then the slant, the weight, the speed, the spacing between words, the general shape or style of handwriting, and next the three zones or levels are carefully examined. And only then is the formation of individual letters studied.

No one sign can be taken as conclusive; as with all forms of character analysis, it is the overall picture, made up of all the signs working together, which counts. Note also that people write in different ways under different circumstances: scrawling a note to the milkman, writing a letter to a friend or lover, applying for a job, making a fair copy for public display – all are different, but a graphologist claims to be able to identify them all as being from the one hand.

Margins

If the writer has been instructed to leave wide margins all around (for example, in an examination paper), this does not apply as much. Similarly, journalists and other professional writers may automatically leave wide margins.

No margins at all may mean that the writer wants to fill every bit of his life (and everybody else's) with himself, or he may be mean, or he may feel rather trapped.

Well-balanced margins could show a well-balanced mind.

A very wide left margin can show a fear of contact or a lack of caution.

A very narrow left margin can show cautiousness and economy, perhaps stinginess.

A left margin that grows wider down the page can

Above: Graphologists are called in to authenticate documents in a wide variety of situations. Here a graphologist examines a court document from the heresy trial of Joan of Arc.

Right: *The Metropolitan Police of London issued this poster in 1886 in an attempt to track down the infamous murderer, Jack the Ripper. The police hoped that his acquaintances would recognize his distinctive style of handwriting.*

show someone who is forward-looking, or becoming less cautious in life.

A left margin that grows narrower can show a developing caution.

A very wide right margin might show a fear of the future.

No space at all on the right might show that the writer is bubbly and effervescent.

The slope

The slope of the lines, including variations in the sloping, might simply show that the paper was badly positioned for the writer. The following are possible indications, but by no means invariable.

If the lines are horizontal (on unlined paper) it could show a clear and orderly mind.

If the lines slope upwards it can show optimism, ambition and enthusiasm.

If they slope downwards it might show pessimism and discouragement, or simply that the writer is tired.

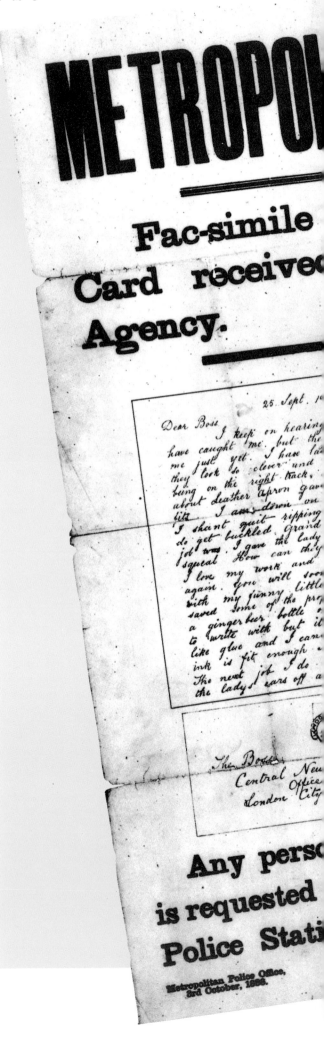

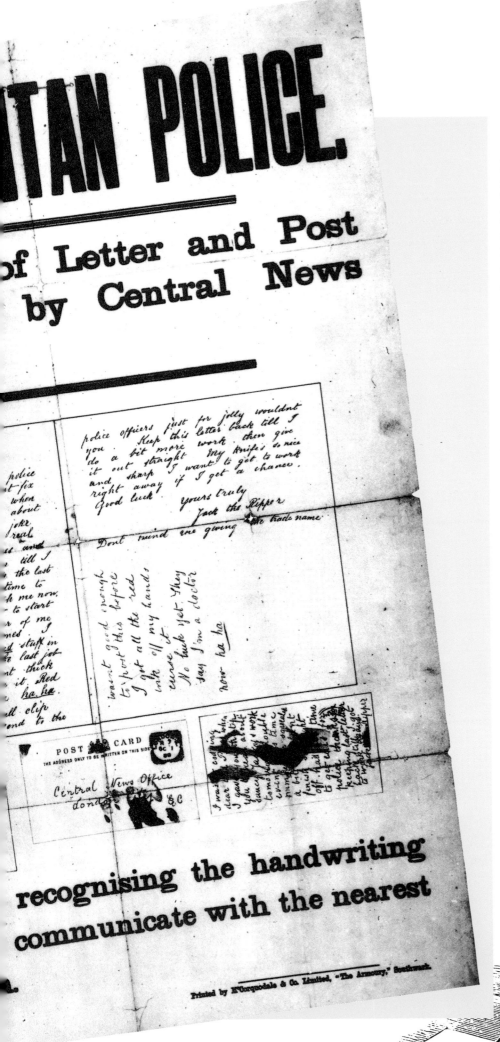

If they rise then fall, so they are hump-shaped, it might show someone who has initial enthusiasms, but no persistence.

If they fall, then rise, it could be that the writer is discouraged, but is determined to stick it through.

If they undulate, they might denote an unstable character, or someone who is always battling against life's problems.

Size

Large writing can show an ambitious and expansive personality, full of confidence and enthusiasm; this can also indicate someone who is proud, arrogant and domineering.

Small writing can show someone who is intelligent and tidy-minded, but quiet and withdrawn, not wanting to draw attention to herself.

Connections

In continuous writing it is very rare that *all* the letters are joined up. Groups of three, four or five letters show mainly positive characteristics, though poor grouping may indicate a disconnected state of mind. Consistency and phraseology are more important than the actual numbers of letters connected.

If words are connected, it can show inventiveness, someone whose thoughts are ahead of the pen, but if overdone it can show carelessness and lack of precision.

Slant

Generally, upright writing can show independence, straightness and self-control.

Slanting forwards can show a creative mind, often extrovert. If extreme it might show someone out of control, probably over-emotional.

Slanting backwards can show reserve, pride or introversion. If extreme it may indicate someone who feels isolated, wrapped up in himself or repressing his emotions.

Weight

A strong hand can show energy, but this also depends on the speed and dynamism of the writing in general.

Too heavy a hand, leaving a deep impression or even slashing at the paper, might show someone not fully in control of himself or of his emotions, and possibly full of his own self-importance. This is apparently more often seen in a male hand.

A very soft, light hand can show someone writing with the minimum expense of energy, maybe because of a naturally economical personality or because of weakness and timidity.

Speed

This obviously depends on how skilled at writing the writer is. Slow writing can show someone who simply finds writing difficult – someone partially illiterate, a child, or someone writing in a language (or a script) with which they are not familiar. But in normal cases, slow writing could show someone who is careful and deliberate, or perhaps unsure of himself.

Fast writing might show confidence and spontaneity, but can denote sloppiness and lack of attention to detail.

Spacing

This will vary to some extent throughout a piece of writing, depending partly on the sense of the words themselves. The average space left between words is usually about the width of a wide letter. Very wide spacing might show a sense of isolation from other people, possibly through pride, aloofness or snobbery.

Very narrow spacing could show warmth and spontaneity, but also perhaps a clinging person, who needs other people a little too much.

Style

Although schoolchildren through the years have had particular handwriting styles hammered into them, by the time they reach their teens they may be making a rounded style more pointed, or vice versa; they may be adding ornamentation to a plain style, or simplifying the more ornate style

they were taught. Graphologists look particularly at how letters are joined, because this is where individuality most alters a taught hand.

Garland is the most simple, easy form of connection in rounded writing; it might show a receptive, friendly person.

Arcade connections are fussier. The writer makes a point of showing the connections, often swooping over the top of the next letter before forming it. It might show someone who is conscious of their position, who is perhaps somewhat guarded, reserved, maybe formal, but courteous.

Angular writing could show firmness, reliability and persistence, someone who will get a job done properly, whatever the inconvenience.

Double-curve writing is a mixture of arcade and garland, looks like a ribbon waving across the paper, and seems to be full of "m"s, "n"s, "u"s and "w"s. If the writing is otherwise energetic and intelligent it might easily show diplomacy and adaptability, but in a weak hand it might show irresolution.

Thread writing sprawls, often untidily, across the paper. It can show a fast-thinking, creative person, but it could mean a capricious, changeable, even hysterical personality.

Zones

Letters, and lines of writing, can be divided into three zones: upper, middle and lower. The middle zone is the vertical space taken up by a lower case "a" or "o", or the rounded part of a "d" or "p"; the upper zone is the ascenders, or upright stalks, of the written letters "b", "d", "f", "h", "k", "l" and "t"; the lower zone is the descenders, or downward strokes, of the written letters "f", "g", "j", "p", "q", "y" and sometimes "z". Note that in handwriting the letter "f" usually has both an ascender and a descender.

The middle zone shows our everyday concept of self, how we fit into the world, our social attitudes and normal emotions.

The upper zone shows our ambitions, imagination, flights of fancy and whim, quests and spiritual awareness.

The lower zone shows our materialism and sensuality, the earthier side of our personality and our emotions.

Ideally the three zones should be of similar

Identifying connections in writing

A

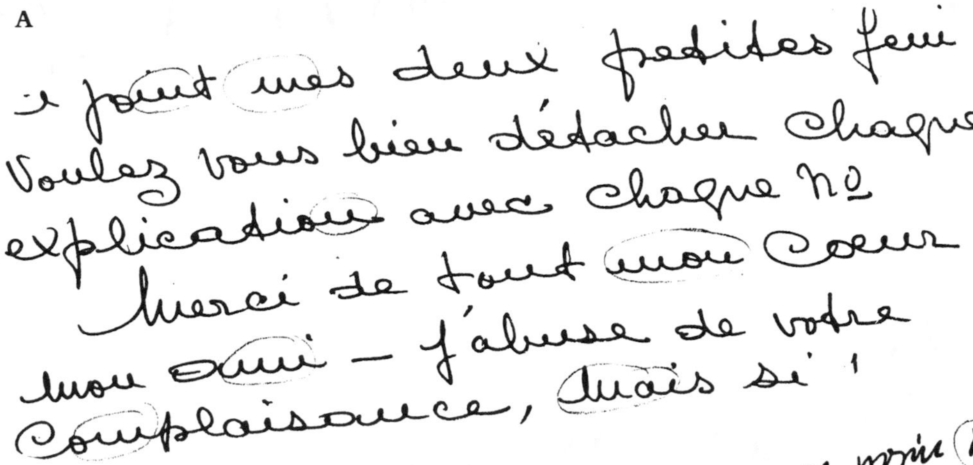

B

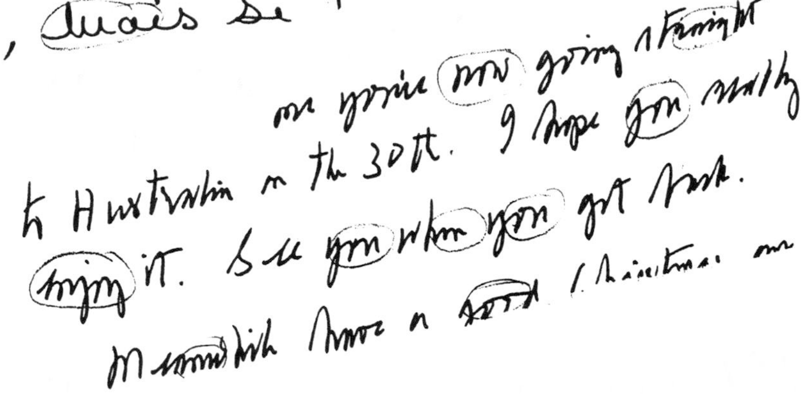

C

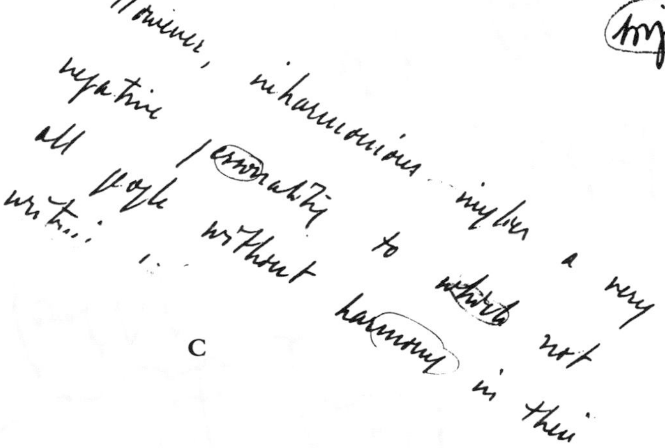

D

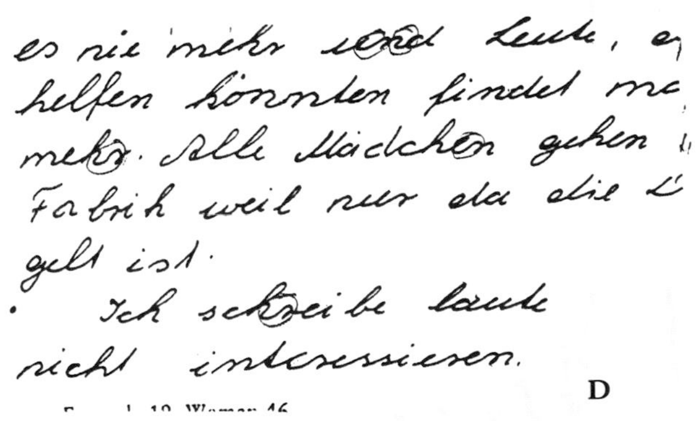

E

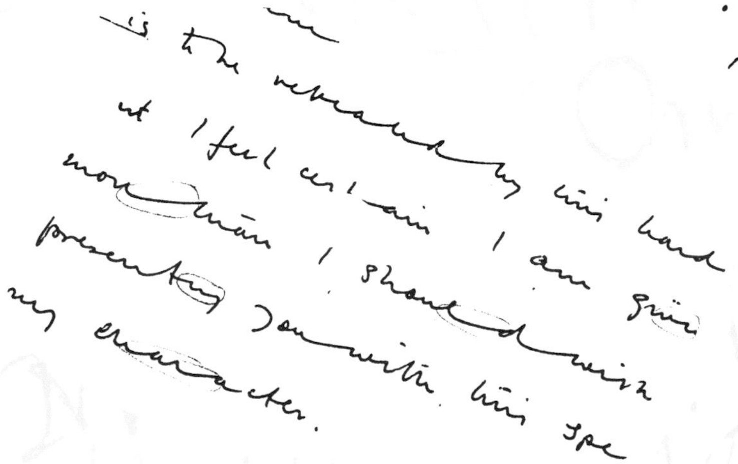

Various styles of handwriting can be identified by the connections made between letters, or even between words. Here are examples of distinct types: A=Garlands, B=Arcades, C=Angular, D=Double Curve, E=Thread or Freeform.

heights, whatever the overall size of the handwriting: the mythical well-balanced person.

Large and small here represent size in relation to the other zones.

A large middle zone can show someone who is solidly at the centre of their own world.

A small middle zone might show a lack of self-confidence or self-awareness.

A large upper zone could show someone who is reaching as far as they can, possibly spiritually-orientated, maybe an habitual day-dreamer.

A small upper zone could show a lack of imagination, a lack of striving after higher things.

A large lower zone might show someone very sensually-orientated, maybe with an appetite for home comforts (and therefore money), good food and wine, and sex; alternatively someone who is very physical, such as a sportsman or a dancer.

A small lower zone might therefore show sexual inhibitions, or a non-physical person.

Individual letters

Graphologists who work with the latin alphabet concentrate particularly on letters such as "d" and "g" with their ascenders and descenders, their connectivity and their propensity for loops; "i" and "t" quite literally for dotting the "i"s and

crossing the "t"s; and the personal capital "I" (in the English language), which in itself can tell a great deal about how the writer views his or her own character.

However, no one indicator of character should ever be taken in isolation; a careful graphologist will spend many hours and sometimes days building up an overall picture of someone's character from handwriting, taking all indicators into consideration, and balancing out contradictions.

Differences in interpretation

The precise "meaning" of any one characteristic of handwriting might vary from place to place in a piece of writing, depending on its immediate context. A graphologist might decide that a characteristic that usually means one thing might mean another in an individual person's handwriting, because of other factors.

A large loop in a lower-case "g", for example, might imply romanticism or earthiness, or it might indicate showiness in another person's hand; it could reveal an imbalance in character if it does not fit in with the rest of the handwriting.

In addition to this, different graphologists, and their textbooks, seem to find different meanings in the same characteristics. This could partly be because the "science" of graphology has developed considerably in the last couple of decades.

Differences of opinion might also stem from different countries; handwriting styles and habits are not the same in every country, and a graphologist from one country cannot pronounce on the writing of someone from another country with anywhere near the same degree of accuracy, until he has immersed himself completely in the writing of that country.

A good graphologist will also constantly be revising his techniques in the light of experience; if he finds a hundred cases of insensitive and unimaginative people displaying signs he has always interpreted as sensitivity, imagination, brightness and artistic creativity, then he should take a good look at his interpretation of these characteristics. Of course, at times, graphologists disagree simply because they hold different opinions. As in other forms of character analysis, intuition combined with knowledge and study holds the key to much of interpretation.

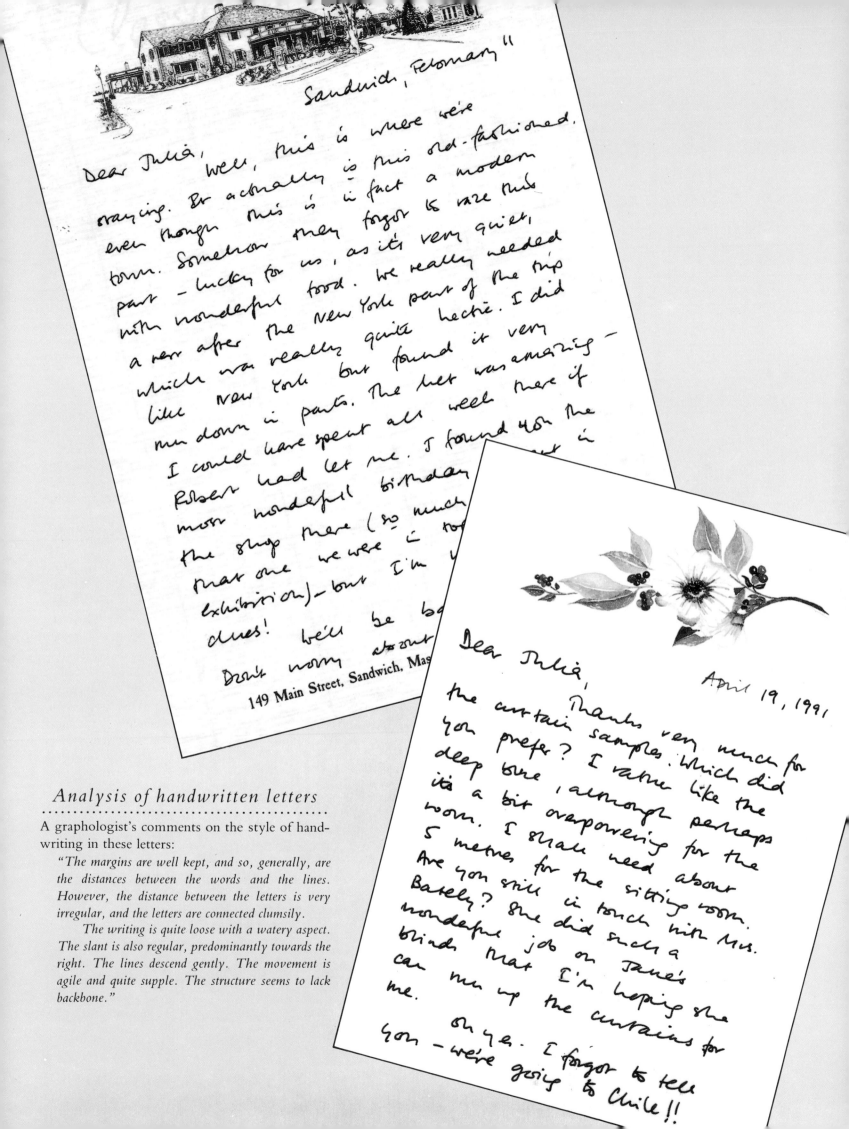

Sandwich, February 11

Dear Julia,
Well, this is where we're
staying. And actually is this old-fashioned,
even though this is in fact a modern
town. Somehow they forgot to raze this
part - lucky for us, as it's very quiet,
with wonderful food. We really needed
a rest after the New York part of the trip
which was really quite hectic. I did
like New York but found it very
run down in parts. The Met was amazing -
I could have spent all week there if
Robert had let me. I found you the
most wonderful birthday [...] in
the shop there (so much [...]
that one we were in [...]
exhibition) - but I'm [...]
clues!   We'll be ba[...]
Don't worry about [...]

149 Main Street, Sandwich, Mas[...]

April 19, 1991

Dear Julia,
Thanks very much for
the curtain samples. Which did
you prefer? I rather like the
deep tone, although perhaps
it's a bit overpowering for the
room. I shall need about
5 metres for the sitting room.
Are you still in touch with Mrs.
Bately? She did such a
wonderful job on Jane's
blinds that I'm hoping she
can run up the curtains for
me.   Oh yes. I forgot to tell
you - we're going to Chile!!

Analysis of handwritten letters

A graphologist's comments on the style of handwriting in these letters:

"The margins are well kept, and so, generally, are
the distances between the words and the lines.
However, the distance between the letters is very
irregular, and the letters are connected clumsily.

The writing is quite loose with a watery aspect.
The slant is also regular, predominantly towards the
right. The lines descend gently. The movement is
agile and quite supple. The structure seems to lack
backbone."

Above: Our signatures are our most revealing marks. We can alter them only with great determination and practice; to a graphologist they provide tremendous insight into our characters and personality traits.

Signatures

The signature is different from a writer's other handwriting. A page of writing can be about anything – work, study notes, holidays, hobbies, friends, memories, plans, and so on – but a signature is "about" the writer. Each signature is its writer's personal statement to the world: "This is who I am; this is how I want to be perceived by you, the reader."

But do our signatures always say what we want them to? Although one may quite consciously develop one's signature so that it looks attractive, strong, or interesting, it will also contain many clues from the subconscious, revealing secrets to the trained eye that the writer would probably prefer were kept hidden.

Although the signature stands apart from the writer's other handwriting, it must also be compared with it; they are, after all, written by the same person, and any major discrepancy shows a conflict between the "true" character and the public persona of the writer. The signature is quite likely to be a little larger than the rest of the writing, but should not be disproportionately so; similarly, although it is often a little fancier, it should not leap out from the rest of the page. For example, a large flourish of a signature following a

page of small, tightly closed-in writing is fairly unusual.

Just as with the rest of handwriting, no one sign should be taken on its own. The graphologist, like any reader, may form from a signature an overall impression of kindliness, quietness, forcefulness, or pretentiousness. However, a careful consideration of a dozen different indicators may reveal to the expert that the writer is forceful, ambitious, thrusting and overbearing, or, on the other hand, is trying to appear forceful while actually being very timid or indecisive.

Generally speaking, it is true to say that a plain, unadorned signature shows the writer to be straightforward, honest and self-confident without being arrogant. Again generally, the more flourishes and fancy strokes, the more affectation and falseness.

If the signature is largely illegible, it can show that the writer has a very low opinion of his own self-importance; or it could show the complete opposite, that he expects everyone to know exactly who he is, and sees no reason why he should take the trouble to reveal himself neatly to people who are less important than himself.

If the signature is much larger than the other writing on the page, it shows that the writer thinks highly of himself, though this is likely to be self-deception; if it is much smaller, it usually shows low self-confidence, without expecting high regard from others.

If the first name is larger than the surname, it shows more informality and a willingness to be friendly; if the surname is larger, it shows a more formal person.

If any part of the signature is underlined, it draws attention to that part of the name and may denote a degree of self-importance. It may well also be compensating for insecurity. Over-tracing of a signature shows nervousness and a lack of self-confidence.

A loop around part of the name, or a large capital letter enclosing some of the rest of the name, reveals a tendency for self-protection, wariness, or sometimes secrecy.

Lines crossing through part of the signature show a self-critical or self-destructive tendency.

A dot at the end can show finality, firmness, pedantry, and a refusal to consider other people's viewpoints.

Left: *Simon Frazer was a partially-educated Victorian working man. Although usually kindly, in a state of somnambulism he killed his baby son, thinking the child was a monster. Note the shakiness of his signature.*

Right: *This is a formal letter from the governor of Durham Gaol notifying the Home Secretary of the impending execution of Mary Ann Cotton for the poisoning of her son. He uses long introductory strokes to some of the words, especially in the phrase "sentenced to be hanged", and, unusually, to the "r" of "Order".*

Bottom: *This is a formal, yet personal statement by Lily May Rouse, the wife of a condemned murderer. She stood by her husband even when his "harem" of lovers around the country was revealed.*

The Great Seers

*P*redictive and divinatory skill is such a strange concept to modern man that almost any lengths are taken to prove it bogus or inaccurate. This is not scepticism, or even cynicism, but just good sense: it is beyond our comprehension, therefore there must be some other explanation.

And yet, in the course of history, there are dozens, if not hundreds, of well-documented cases where accurate predictions have been made, recorded and circulated years before the prophesied event has taken place. There is no argument: this has happened over and over again, and it is only the hyper-rationality of twentieth-century mankind that blinds us to this obvious fact.

Some men and women are undisputedly given the gift of the future: with faith, it is open to all. In this section are noted a few famous examples to illustrate that destiny can be revealed – that it is possible to tear through the veils of time.

Opposite: *This Rembrandt etching shows a magician predicting the future using a magic mirror. The magic qualities of mirrors stem from the early art of hydromancy, foretelling the future by gazing into water. In medieval Europe mirrors were considered lucky in that they kept away evil spirits. Even today mirrors are associated through folklore with predicting the identity of young girls' future husbands.*

Nostradamus

Michel de Notre Dame (or Nostre-Dame according to some sources) was born into the great Jewish community that thrived in Provence during the sixteenth century. Both of his grandfathers were court physicians to King René of Provence – Jean de Saint-Rémy and Pierre de Nostre-Dame: their offspring married, and Michel was born in 1503. He came under the influence of his grandfathers at an early age. At that time physicians would have been well-versed in all of the esoteric and arcane disciplines that were at the fringe of medicine – alchemy and astrology among them – and the boy, tutored in particular by Jean de Saint-Rémy, would have received instruction in these subjects along with his quota of more usual lessons in Latin, Hebrew, mathematics and Greek.

Nostradamus (as we will henceforward call him) completed his basic studies in the Humanities at Avignon, and then, naturally enough, given his family background, moved on to the great medieval University of Montpellier, where he joined the medical school. This was at the time of the black plague in Europe, and much of his early experience came in the treatment and attempted prevention of the disease. As the story goes,

he had an extraordinarily high rate of success compared with his colleagues: his fame spread, and he began to be summoned to the bedsides of the wealthy and influential. At this stage he had still not officially qualified as a doctor – this came later, after the plague had ended, when he returned to Montpellier to take his examinations.

In his healing travels, he had developed a taste for the countryside, and now settled in the small town of Agen, where he married Adriète de Loubéjac, and fathered two sons. Unfortunately all three members of his family died suddenly, and the depressed physician once more took to an itinerant existence. This was a transitional time in his life: most now believe that it was this period of intense grief and existential re-evaluation that transformed a learned but staid physician into the most extraordinary seer and prophet of recorded history. Certainly, little is known of his movements at this time (though it is rumoured that he travelled widely in Italy and France to meet some of the greatest esoteric scholars of the age), but when he returned to view, he was a different man. One story, possibly apocryphal, told of his "missing" period in his life is that while in Italy he mystified his companions by falling prostrate before an undistinguished junior monk. In response to their astonishment, he would say only, "I had to bow before His Holiness". The action only became logical many decades later, when the monk was made a Cardinal, and finally became Pope Sixtus the Fifth in 1585. If true, this is the first recorded exemplification of Nostradamus's divinatory gift.

At the age of forty-four he married for the second time and settled once more in Provence, this time at Salon. He still practised as a physician,

and his reputation and fame were as strong as before. So famous did he become, that the rich and powerful beat a path to his door, and his presence in Salon did a great deal to make it a popular and wealthy town. Yet his great skills, combined with the lifestyle he had adopted, also caused the rumour to spread that he was an occultist and practitioner of witchcraft. Although he was devoutly Catholic (his parents having had to convert to Christianity to comply with the draconian religious laws prevalent in France at the time), he would spend days at a time in his dusty study surrounded by huge and obscure books – the great works of medieval learning – and his magnificent collection of strange instruments, including astrolabes, alembics (glass implements used for distillation), wands, mirrors and other alchemical equipment. It is perhaps no small wonder that the simple folk of Salon misunderstood his purpose: learning in the sixteenth century inevitably encompassed subjects closely associated with the occult.

It was at this time that Nostradamus himself added to the flames of rumour by admitting for the first time that he believed himself to be endowed with the gift of prophecy – that he had been born with an extra sense which allowed him to foretell future events. At the same time, he also made it clear that these prophetic visions did not just visit him at random: he had developed a scientific system which allowed him to enter the future under the right circumstances. The system, together with his inherited sixth sense, combined to allow him to record events yet to take place. To this day, nobody has managed to discover what processes, materials, or substances the system embraced, though many have sought for years to "break the code" of Nostradamus's methods.

One clue may be in Nostradamus's ancestry. His forefathers fled persecution and slaughter as Jewish refugees, and one theory is that, over the generations, old manuscripts and books from the ancient Egyptian libraries may have been passed from father to son until they reached Michel. His grandfather's learning, and the nature of their profession, could well serve to reinforce this argument, as does Nostradamus's own confession that he had learned several ancient Egyptian documents by heart before destroying them. The whereabouts of the knowledge and artefacts from the ancient libraries destroyed by the barbarians is, of course, one of the central preoccupations of all those interested in occultism and the mysterious arts: it has also been associated with the wisdom inherent in the Tarot pack. It is therefore perhaps not surprising that this theme should again have been infiltrated into the story of Nostradamus. Whatever the truth about these rarer books, he is certainly known to have possessed a copy of *De Mysteriis Egyptorum*, Iamblichus's fourth-century esoteric guide, an edition of which was produced in Lyons in 1547.

Whatever the origin of his skills, his proclamation of them, and his demonstration of their veracity, soon made him a wonder of his age. His routine was now set: every night he would sit before a brass bowl filled almost to overflowing with water. He would then record his visions in quatrains (four-line poems). The reading and interpretation of these poems would provide the key to the future. The poems were gathered together in book form and called *Centuries*, and the first edition was published in 1555 (by M. Bonhomme, a printer at Lyons).

The circulation of Nostradamus's verses caused a sensation. They quickly reached all the civilized courts and corners of the world, and became vastly influential. An argument could be made that Nostradamus had become the first "popular" bestselling author in publishing history. Salon, already changed by the influx of notable "tourists" who had come to consult the great physician, was transformed virtually overnight into. one of the most remarkable and famous locations in Christendom. Even the boy King of France, Charles IX, visited Salon, braving a new outbreak of plague in the region, to meet the great prophet.

Nostradamus's fame and success bred jealousy in his rivals, and many pamphlets were published attempting to make him out to be a charlatan. At the same time, the accuracy of his predictions further increased the rumours that he was a witch – and in retrospect, given the atmosphere and attitudes of the time, he was lucky to avoid being officially accused or physically attacked by the mob. He lived on in Salon, revered by some and reviled by others, until he died beside his bench, as he himself had foretold, on the night of 1 July 1566.

The Predictions of Nostradamus

As has been mentioned, great mystery surrounds the work of Nostradamus, and little is known of his methods. The quatrains themselves have provoked enormous controversy over the years. A typical reaction is that "they are so vague they could be applied to any event", and, indeed, it is the case that names are changed, generalizations are common, and the verses often look, on first reading, quite meaningless.

Nostradamus's own explanation for this is simple and reasonable: it is given in the foreword he placed in the second edition of the *Centuries*, in which he dedicates the book to King Henry II. "The danger of the times, O Most Serene Majesty, requires that such hidden events be not manifested save by enigmatic speech: . . . did I so desire, I could fix the time for every quatrain . . . but that it might to some be disagreeable." This implies two additional reasons: firstly, for the most contemporary predictions, Nostradamus feared that knowledge of events in the short term future might provoke unrest or even violence. If someone knows that an invasion is planned, or a war is to take place, that information alone might be enough to put a spark to the flame. And secondly, it clearly touches on the central dilemma of all predictive endeavour: namely the advisability or otherwise of revealing the future, once known, to those whose lives are to be affected. To put it simply, Nostradamus was aware that most people cannot cope with prior knowledge of their own destiny – whether good or bad. It is for this reason that his quatrains are packed with anagrams, slight misspellings and synonyms (Hister for Hitler; Nizaram for Mazarin and so on). For those who doubt, it is interesting to note that one of the most respected mathematicians and statisticians in the world once calculated that the probability of such transpositions being accidental (i.e. that Nostradamus invented random names and references which just happened to closely fit later historical figures) is, on close analysis of the texts, so many millions to one that it is infinite. In other words, there is no statistical chance that Nostradamus's work is bogus.

Students of Nostradamus should not look on the quatrains purely for obvious and direct advice,

Dieu s'ouvert icy de ma bouche.
Pour tánoncer la Verité
Si ma prediction te touche
Rends grace à sa Divinité.

A b o v e : *Michel de Notre Dame, better known as Nostradamus, believed he was endowed with the gift of prophecy. He is pictured here at his desk, surrounded by books and astrological instruments. The verse beneath reinforces the belief that his keen talent is a divine one; he saw himself as God's mouthpiece for the truth.*

but should approach the verses as they would any other type of divinatory reading: the information is provided, but personal analysis and interpretation is the final part of the process. As Le Pelletier, the most distinguished scholar of the quatrains, has noted, they are "a sort of . . . Tarot in verse, a cabbalistic kaleidoscope". Nostradamus, like the great ancient oracles, creates a divinatory framework which, for the sympathetic and mentally-atuned interpreter, lays bare the future: each quatrain is, in those terms, like a cast of the runes or a layout of the Tarot which needs to be read with the same degree of depth and sensitivity to discover the truth. Nostradamus summarized the system succinctly: "To understand my [verses] is as easy as blowing your nose, but the sense is more difficult to grasp".

To take just one example in detail, this is the quatrain most often interpreted as Nostradamus's prediction of Napoleon's rise to political power:

> Un Empereur naistra près d'Italie,
> Qui, à l'Empire, sera vendu bien cher;
> Diront avec quels gens il se ralie,
> Qu'on trouvera moins prince qu boucher.

This is only one of many of the quatrains associated with Napoleon, who lived three hundred years after Nostradamus. Translated, it reads: "An Emperor will be born near Italy, whose empire will cost France very dear. They will say of those who he gathers around him that they are butchers rather than princes". Napoleon was born in Corsica – close to Italy; his expansionist dreams effectively drained and destroyed France, eventually leading to its defeat in a succession of wars; and his generals and political associates were certainly not princely in revolutionary France. The phrase "moins prince" is perhaps the most significant: in Nostradamus's time, the thought of an Empire without princes was unheard of – foreseeing an Empire may be a lucky guess, but foretelling Republicanism is divination almost beyond the realms of imagination. If this were a single prophecy it might be explained away by chance, but there are "Ten Centuries" of quatrains – over one thousand, set in chronological order. It is no wonder that Goethe, in *Faust*, shows his protagonist reading the *Centuries* of Nostradamus and proclaiming, "Was it a god who penned these signs?"

A b o v e : *"The London Senate will put to death its King", decreed Nostradamus, and indeed Charles I was condemned to death for the crime of high treason by his parliament; he was taken to his execution in Whitehall, London, in 1649.*

L e f t : *Nostradamus's gift of predicting events was uncannily accurate; he prophesied the destruction of the great force of the Armada sent by Spain against the British. The British fleet was led by Sir Francis Drake in 1588 and victory was swift.*

Left: *The description of Nostradamus's "Empereur", mentioned in one of his Centuries, fits the figure of Napoleon with astonishing accuracy. Napoleon has been the subject of much esoteric analysis, particularly that of numerology; having been connected with the prophecies of Nostradamus he remains a fascinating figure for the application of other forms of predictive research.*

The Astonishing Accuracy of Nostradamus's Verses

Nostradamus's quatrains are now thought to have accurately predicted the following events and circumstances, among hundreds of others:

★ *The blinding and death of King Henry II of France*

★ *The ascension to the throne of France of all three of Henry II's sons – Francis II, Charles IX, and Henry III*

★ *The Spanish Armada and its destruction by the English*

★ *An English colonial Empire of three hundred years, commencing in the last quarter of the sixteenth century, and beginning to deteriorate at the end of the nineteenth century*

★ *The French Revolution*

★ *The English Civil War ("The London Senate will put to death its King")*

★ *The life and achievements of Oliver Cromwell ("Twenty months he will hold the Kingdom in utter power. A dictator, cruel, but leaving a worse cruelty behind")*

★ *The scandals of the reign of Louis XV ("The great monarch who will succeed . . . will give an example of an immoral and adulterous life")*

★ *The atrocities and carnage in Nantes in 1793, when over one thousand people were slaughtered*

★ *The harnessing of electricity for man's use, and the coming of telegraphic and wireless communications*

★ *The world-wide 'flu epidemic of 1918–1919*

★ *The rise of Hitler and the Third Reich in Germany*

★ *The political power of Charles de Gaulle in France*

★ *The atom bombs dropped on Hiroshima and Nagasaki at the end of World War II in the Far East ("At the port and in two cities, two scourges such as have never been seen")*

★ *The assassination of two of the Kennedy brothers, John and Robert, and the political demise of the third, Edward*

Above and left: *The rise to power of Hitler and the German Third Reich was foretold by Nostradamus in his collection of poems, Centuries. The reference that is relevant to Hitler is actually spelt "Hister", yet, statistically speaking, the probability of the similarity being mere coincidence has been found to be nearly impossible.*

Right: *The extensive use of electricity was also foretold by Nostradamus; Thomas Alva Edison invented the incandescent lamp and brought electric light to many millions of homes.*

Cheiro

A b o v e : *The American author Mark Twain was facing bankruptcy when he was told by Cheiro that he would receive a great sum of money when he reached the age of sixty-eight. Although he received this prophecy with scepticism, he did indeed enter into a lucrative publishing contract exactly as predicted by Cheiro.*

Count Louis Hamon was born in Ireland in 1866. Moving to London, and adopting the pseudonym Cheiro, by the 1890s he had established himself as the darling of society and the most famous palm reader in the world. He was fortunate, in that his appearance on the scene coincided with an enormous upsurge in the popularity of and interest in predictive skills, but he takes credit for having the looks, charm, and genuine divinatory talent to take full advantage of the mood of the times. The books he published at the time, some of which are still available, were instant successes, and he also made a series of films for the early cinema on the subject of chiromancy. His personal history remains hazy – leading to the feeling among some that he was no more than a con-man who made more than his fair share of lucky guesses. However, as can be seen from the list of just some of his predictions given here, statistical probability sides with Cheiro in confirming that his work was much more than opportunistic flammery.

One of the best descriptions of Cheiro's fame comes in the "Publishers' Preface" to his early work *Read Your Past Present and Future*; though hardly likely to be completely objective, all of the examples given are confirmed by other sources.

"The name 'Cheiro' covers one of the most remarkable personalities of modern times, a highly-gifted man who, had he desired, might have won fame in many other pursuits in life, but who chose at the very threshold of his manhood to live in the East, so that he might be able to study the forgotten wisdom of those wonderful races such as the Hindus, the Chinese and Persians, and returning to Western civilisation he took a sacred vow that for twenty years he would devote himself to converting the most intellectual and highest personages in the world to believe in the strange Science of which he had made himself the Master.

In carrying out his vow his success has been phenomenal. He has read and taken impressions of the hands of most of the crowned heads of Europe, together with Presidents of Republics and Kings of Commerce. One and all have borne witness that 'Cheiro's' powers of predicting events years in advance from the lines in

R i g h t : *Cheiro's best-selling book on the predictive strengths of palm-reading. Some of his works are still available today and his followers are dedicated and widespread.*

HUNDRED THOUSANDTH EDITION.

READ YOUR PAST · PRESENT AND FUTURE

BY CHEIRO

PRICE 1/-

their hands has been something akin to the marvellous.

Taking one or two illustrations at random: 'Cheiro' predicted the date of Queen Victoria's death, the exact year and even the month when King Edward the VII would pass away, the terrible destiny that awaited the late Czar of Russia, the assassination of King Humbert of Italy, the attempt on the Shah's life in Paris, and in thousands of well-known persons' lives with equal accuracy, the leading events of their careers.

It is on record that one of the most dramatic predictions ever made, was, when in 1894 (twenty-two years before the tragic event) 'Cheiro' foretold to Lord Kitchener the exact year of his death – and *the likely form it would take*. The words of this remarkable prediction made by 'Cheiro' at the War Office, was the following:

'That he, Kitchener, would meet his death in his sixty-sixth year – not the end that a Soldier might naturally expect on the battle-field – but that his death would be caused by water, most probably by storm or disaster at Sea, with the attendant chance of some form of capture by an enemy and exile from which he would never recover.'

Above: *Lord Kitchener in the now-famous poster appealing for army recruits. In 1894 Cheiro examined a palm print given to him by Kitchener and predicted his death by drowning in 1916.*

When this prediction was made – the great Kitchener was only a plain Colonel and in that year 1894 he gave 'Cheiro' a signed impression of his hand which had strangely enough the Seal of the War Office imprinted on it, which may be seen at the top of the second finger in the Film reproduction of Kitchener's hand, which is now being shown at all the principal Cinemas in England.

Lord Kitchener never forgot this prediction. During the Great War, while at the Front, as related in the Press, he mentioned it to General de Ballincourt and members of his Staff.

The tragic sinking of the battleship 'Hampshire' on the evening of the 5th June, 1916, in Lord Kitchener's sixty-sixth year, and the chance that the great Soldier might have been captured by an enemy submarine, bore out 'Cheiro's' prediction to the letter, and is a remarkable example of the accuracy of his system in reading the lines of the hand.

A similar prediction was made by 'Cheiro' to the celebrated journalist, W.T. Stead, and with equal exactness, when he went to his death in the disaster to the 'Titanic' on her first voyage.

It can be said without exaggeration, that 'Cheiro' has become world-famous through the perfection to which he had brought this Study of the Hand. In London, Paris, New York, Boston, Chicago, in all the great Towns of America, in Petrograd, Rome and the principal Continental cities, he has demonstrated that the lines of the hand are a veritable chart of life, his success has been certified to by all classes and in his Visitor's Book autographed testimonies may be seen that are *without a parallel* in the history of the World.

In this small but concise work that we now issue to the public, the reader will find clearly drawn illustrations of the various lines that seem so bewildering when glanced at in ignorance of their real meaning. The Author, however, illuminates the whole subject in a lucid style peculiarly his own, and in such a form that the reader can 'Know Himself' or Herself, in a way that would be impossible by any other study.

We have no hesitation in saying that this book places in concise form rare knowledge that cannot but be found of benefit to all."

Predictions by Cheiro

★ *Mark Twain records that in 1895, when he was sixty, Cheiro told him in a reading that he (Twain) would suddenly come into money in his sixty-eighth year. Bankrupt at the time, and in debt to the tune of over $90,000, Twain viewed this with amusement. But in November 1903 he was, out of the blue, offered a contract with Harper, the publisher, which cleared his debts and ensured him thereafter an income of over $100,000 per annum.*

★ *He accurately predicted to King Edward VII that he would die in his sixty-ninth year. He also accurately foresaw the time of Queen Victoria's death, and told others of his prediction.*

★ *In an exhibition reading at which he was unaware of the identity of his subjects (being separated by a cloth screen), he told Oscar Wilde that he was a well-known man at the height of his fame, but that he must avoid rash actions in seven years' time or he would be ruined. Seven years later, Wilde was jailed, after two infamous legal actions which he himself initiated, for homosexuality.*

★ *He visited Russia in 1904 to do a reading for the Czar in which he foretold that Russia would be involved in a calamitous war between 1914– 1917 and that the Czar would then lose all he loved most.*

★ *His most famous and well-documented prediction was in a reading for Lord Kitchener, over twenty years beforehand, that he would die by drowning in 1916 unless he avoided all forms of sea travel. Kitchener went down on the Hampshire in 1916 during World War I.*

★ *He told the killer, Meyer, when he was on death row that he would not be executed as his life line continued for many more years. This seemed impossible at that time, but, sure enough, Meyer received a last minute reprieve.*

Below: Among the many famous people who consulted Cheiro were film stars such as Lillian Gish, left, and Mary Pickford. Cheiro's fame was such that he attracted a rich clientele from among the ranks of the great social circles of the time.

William Lilly

William Lilly (1602–1681) was the most famous and revered astrologer of his time. Born shortly after the death of John Dee, he followed in Dee's

Right: An enigmatic portrait of William Lilly, great astrologer of the seventeenth century. He is pictured here with an astrological chart and a book of zodiacal symbols. Suspended in the heavens behind him hangs a zodiacal sphere.

tradition, and was one of the last of the great "occult" astrologers. He was closely aligned to the Parliamentarian cause in the English Civil War, and lost his patronage and fell out of favour when the Monarchy was reinstated.

Lilly's divinations were expressed in the form of mystical symbolic drawings and astrological pamphlets. His two most famous predictions were of the Great Plague in 1665 and the Great Fire of London in 1666: both predictions were made ten years before the events he accurately described, and were recorded and circulated at the time of prediction.

Lilly, the Great Plague, and the Great Fire of London

Lilly's book of *Astrological Predictions*, published in 1648, contains the following passage:

"In the year 1656 the Aphelium of Mars, who is the general signification of England, will be in Virgo, which is assuredly the ascendant of the English monarchy, but Aries of the King-dom. When this absis therefore, of Mars, shall appear in Virgo, who shall expect less than a strange catastrophe of human affairs in the commonwealth, monarchy, and Kingdom of England? There will then, either in or about these times, or near that year, or within ten years more or less of that time, appear in this kingdom so strange a revolution of fate, so grand a catastrophe and great mutation unto this monarchy and government, as never yet appeared; of which as the times now stand, I have no liberty or encouragement to deliver my opinion, – only, it will be ominous to London, unto her merchants at sea, to her traffique on land, to her poor, to all sorts of people inhabit-ing in her or her liberties, by reason of sundry fires and a consuming plague."

In 1651 Lilly published a pamphlet called *Monarchy and no Monarchy* containing one of his famous symbolic woodcuts within which, to quote his autobiography, "[I had] framed an hieroglyphic . . . representing a great sickness and mortality; wherein you may see the representation of people in their winding-sheets, persons digging graves and sepulcures, coffins etc. . . . After the coffins

Below: Gatherings of the Spiritualist movement, of which Davis was a devotee, were very popular in the mid-nineteenth century and attracted authors such as Edgar Allen Poe and Arthur Conan Doyle.

and pickaxes there is a representation of a great city all in flames of fire."

Lilly was still alive when the plague and fire had happened. So famous and notorious did he become, that the Parliamentary Committee examining the causes of the fire summoned him to give evidence, suggesting that he may have been responsible for starting the fire in order to make his predictions come true. He told the Parliamentarians that his foresight was based purely on astrological skill – an explanation which was accepted.

Andrew Jackson Davis

Davis, the first great American seer, was born in Orange County, New York, in 1826 into an impoverished farming family. From infancy there are records of his visions and the voices he heard – it seems that he was born with the gift of clairvoyance. This may have been refined when, in 1843, a travelling mesmerist visited Davis's community and helped Davis to develop and work on

---

The Predictions of Andrew Jackson Davis

In 1856, on the Railway:
Cars may be constructed so that no accident or even collision would be dangerous to either passengers or baggage . . . Instead of the present gallery-looking cars, we will have spacious saloons, almost portable dwellings, moving with such speed that perhaps there will be advertisements – "Through to California in four days!"

In 1856, on motor vehicles:
Carriages and travelling saloons [will move along] country roads – sans horse, sans steam, sans any visible motive power, moving with greater speed and safety than at present. Carriages will be moved by a strange and beautiful and simple admixture of aqueous and atmospheric gases – so easily condensed, so simply ignited, and so imparted by a machine . . . as to be entirely concealed between the forward wheels.

In 1856, on air travel:
It will not only [be] the locomotive on the rail, and the carriage on the country road, but aerial cars, also, which will move through the sky from country to country.

---

the ability to enter trance-like states. Soon Davis's parochial fame spread, and he began to travel around the country holding clairvoyant seminars and giving *ad hoc* exhibitions of his divinatory skills.

By 1845 he was publishing books which were dictated while he was entranced – almost speaking in tongues. The view at the time was that the subjects of his books were of such an erudite and esoteric mixture of material that it was impossible that the words came from the relatively uneducated Davis. He would discourse, for example, on advanced medical theories which challenged even the most up-to-date knowledge of research physicians, and one of his specialities was to diagnose and cure disease, without ever having received any formal training.

His books also contained fantastical prophecies of things unheard of and unenvisaged at the time. Having seen him lecture, the visionary writer Edgar Allen Poe became a follower, and was convinced of the veracity of his foresight. Others have not been so sure, and one body of critics has always been highly suspicious of Davis's work and his motives – no more so than when, in later years, Davis became emersed in the Spiritualist movement, which at that time was riddled with con-men and charlatans. Nevertheless, Davis stands head and shoulders above his contemporaries in terms of the accuracy of what he predicted: his words were written, recorded, and published at the time, and, as can be seen clearly from the quoted highlights here, there is no disputing their accuracy.

Left : In 1651 Lilly predicted the Great Fire of London which devastated the city in 1666; he saw it as following a period of grief and sickness – the Black Death. This prophecy was proved true within his lifetime – and he was regarded with great suspicion.

Left : Hailed as one of the great American prophets, Andrew Jackson Davis soon established a strong reputation for prediction through the publication of his books and while conducting lecture tours around the country.

A b o v e : *One of the Oracles of Delphi in a frenzied, trance-like state which would enable her to pronounce on the future of those who consulted her.*

R i g h t : *Socrates, the great Greek philosopher, drinking hemlock after being found guilty of impious behaviour towards the gods, in spite of having been declared the wisest man alive by the Oracle.*

The Oracle at Delphi

This is not one seer, but hundreds: the Oracles – usually young women, called sibyls – who maintained the oracular tradition at the temples of Greece for hundreds of years. Of these temples the most famous and revered was at Delphi, and the sibyl at Delphi was always called Pythia.

People would travel for weeks to get to the Oracle and ask a question. The Oracle would normally appear only once every month, and the fees charged were enormous, meaning that only the rich and aristocratic could make use of the service. Once paid, the Oracle would enter a frenzied trance state, in which she would become a link for the voices of the gods. It is claimed that to aid the trance Pythia used drugs: possibly a mixture of the sacred waters of Cassotis, crushed bay leaf and a natural gas emanating from the rock crevices surrounding the site.

The Oracle and Socrates

The Oracle at Delphi, asked who was the wisest man alive, pronounced that it was Socrates. As the Oracle could not be wrong, this was accepted as fact, and it was this elevation of Socrates among his brethren in those democratic times that first set his countrymen against him, and resulted, eventually, in his forced suicide.

This was genuinely a case of speaking in tongues: the messages were histrionic, garbled, and colourful, providing, like the later quatrains of Nostradamus, a medium for the message rather than the message itself. The last stage in the process was the interpretation of the Oracle's enigmatic pronouncements.

B e l o w : *The remains of the Temple of Apollo in Delphi, Greece. Situated high on a hillside in an isolated area of the Greek mainland, the site still retains its rich atmosphere of mystery.*

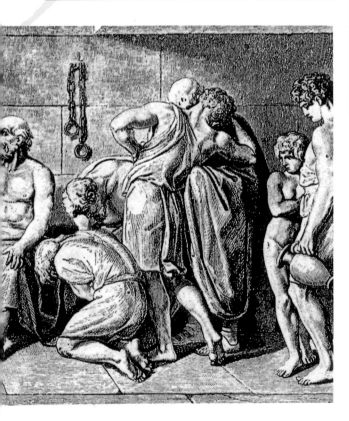